D0130811

The Broadway Song Companion

*An Annotated Guide to Musical
Theatre Literature by
Voice Type and Song Style*

David P. DeVenney

The Scarecrow Press, Inc.
Lanham, Md., & London
1998

SCARECROW PRESS, INC.

Published in the United States of America
by Scarecrow Press, Inc.
4720 Boston Way
Lanham, Maryland 20706

British Library Cataloguing in Publication Information Available

Library of Congress Cataloging-in-Publication Data

DeVenney, David P., 1958–
    The Broadway song companion : an annotated guide to musical
theatre literature by voice type and song style / David P. DeVenney.
        p.   cm.
    Includes bibliographical references and indexes.
    ISBN 0-8108-3373-5 (cloth : alk. paper)
    1. Musicals—Bibliography. 2. Popular music—Bibliography.
3. Voice types (Singing) —Handbooks, manuals, etc.   I. Title.
ML128.M78D48   1998
0.16.782'4—dc21   97-42486
                                                      CIP
                                                       MN

0-8108-3373-5

♾ ™ The paper used in this publication meets the minimum requirements of
American National Standard for Information Sciences—Permanence of
Paper for Printed Library Materials, ANSI Z39.48–1984.
Manufactured in the United States of America.

for Bob

Contents

Foreword

This book began as a private resource for myself and my students and eventually evolved into the volume that you find in your hands. For thirteen years I served on the music faculty at Otterbein College, where many of my principal duties involved teaching our musical theatre students. One of those responsibilities was helping to plan senior cabaret recitals, designed to demonstrate a student's familiarity performing musical theatre selections of all styles and periods, providing a capstone experience to his or her four years of study.

After years of helping them search for appropriate music, I finally became frustrated trying to remember what song came from which musical, what its range was, and whether or not it might be the right type of song for their voices or their cabaret requirements. Thus I began this project: to go through my own collection of scores and categorize the songs by voice type, range, and style. As I discussed the idea with my colleagues, they were uniformly supportive about the project, since all of them had performed similar searches countless times. In sum, this book was born both of frustration and from the idea that there ought to be a practical guide to the great body of musical theatre songs, making them more readily accessible to performers.

The Broadway Song Companion lists well over two thousand song titles from more than 210 musicals, both early and late, both popular shows and those that were short-lived, from both on- and off-Broadway. The main purposes of this study have been to identify and label solo literature; to identify excerptable duets, trios, quartets, and other ensemble pieces; and finally to provide a listing of other material in these shows, because doing so might be useful to directors, producers, and others who have need for a quick reference to this information.

I have designed this book primarily with the singing actor in mind. A tenor suited to character parts, for example, may need to know whether or not a particular show has a part for him before he takes time out of a busy schedule to audition. A quick glance at one of the shows included here should give him that information. A mezzo looking for a good ballad to fill out a cabaret act she is working on will also find several dozen song choices listed here. A soprano and bass looking for a good trio to perform with a tenor will also find literature suited to their purposes.

Directors and producers may also find this book helpful. A director seeking information while planning an upcoming season, knowing the makeup and nature of the company he or she has hired, can browse at leisure through these pages and find any number of shows that might fit the bill. Similarly, directors who have a good chorus but limited suitable leading players will be able to find shows, both familiar and forgotten, that might fit their casts.

Several caveats need to be mentioned. First, nearly half of these shows have been annotated using published piano-vocal scores, available for perusal in public libraries and sometimes for purchase. These published scores may differ in slight ways from materials that are distributed by rental companies. Secondly, "vocal selections" books are notoriously different from both publisher's parts and rental materials. Only full scores have been used to provide the annotations in this volume, and the reader should not be surprised if the version of a song he knows is in a different key or a different arrangement in the vocal selections book he may own. Finally, cast albums of shows may be in yet another key, and frequently contain arrangements of music made to fit the requirements of the recording. While helpful in general, they may differ in significant ways from the actual music of a show, a fact the actor or director should keep in mind.

While many agents loaned rental materials for annotation here, several shows were not available for reasons of royalty arrangements, part preparation, and so forth, at the time of this compilation. Furthermore, some popular shows, particularly those by Andrew Lloyd Webber, are closely held and difficult to come by. While I have made every effort to be inclusive, certain shows may now be available that were not at the time I wrote this book.

With this said, it is my hope that this book will prove useful and valuable to a large number of singers, actors, voice teachers, directors, and producers. My aim has been to provide the user with a complete, accurate, handy compendium of data that will offer access to a body of literature much loved, but often difficult to access. If I have been successful, this great, fascinating music will have been served.

Many people and organizations contributed to this guide, and it is only right to acknowledge them here. Craig Johnson, my colleague from Otterbein College, was very encouraging at the outset of this research, as were my students, especially Bob Cline, Dan Hughes, Johnny Steiner, and Catherine Smart. Dan Yurgaitis and Dick Hansen, the two members of the musical theatre faculty at The University of Arizona, were both helpful in the extreme, and provided scores from their libraries as well as suggestions and encouragement. My friend Josef Knott provided a summer's respite for proofreading on Cape Cod.

Most of the research was undertaken at the Courtwright Memorial Library of Otterbein College, The Ohio State University Music and Dance Library, the Columbus (Ohio) Public Library, The University of Arizona Music Library, and the New York Public Library for the Performing Arts at Lincoln Center. I would like to extend my thanks to the respective staffs of these institutions. Finally, I would like to thank the three principal rental agents for the loan of scores and the gentlemen who answered my queries for help with generosity and dispatch: Mr. Jim Merrillat of Music Theatre International, Mr. Brad Lorenz of Samuel French, Inc., and Mr. Peter Hut of Tams-Witmark Music Library, Inc. All provided scores free of charge, without which many of the more recent musicals would not have been included here. Finally, I would like to thank my good friend David DeCooman, who did some research for me, and who, as always, provided unflagging personal support.

Guide to Use

This *Companion* is designed to provide a quick-reference guide to the solos, duets, trios, and ensemble music of the Broadway musical. Shows appear alphabetically, with the year of their premiere or composition and the names of the composer and lyricist. Each song annotated is listed in show order, followed by the name of the character who sings it. When a character's name first appears, it is also identified by voice part (soprano, mezzo, tenor, baritone, or bass; abbreviated as S, M, T, Bar, B). The next column lists the exact vocal range according to the following octave method, where middle C is c1:

C to B   c to b   c1 (middle c) to b1   c2 to b2   c3 to b3

Vocal ranges are inclusive, meaning that they include opening recitative sections as well, which in practice might not be excerpted when performed outside the context of a show. When two or more characters sing a given number, their vocal ranges are given in the order in which they sing, separated by a slash (/).

In the third column of each annotation, I have given a style or tempo designation. These fall into three broad categories: ballads, uptempo numbers, and character pieces. A number is often given more than one parameter. An uptempo song might also be a character piece, and will be so labeled. Likewise, a number may be uptempo, but move a bit slower than usual; it would be labeled "mod. [moderate] uptempo." A ballad that moves along somewhat might be defined as a "moving ballad" or a "moderate ballad"; there are also pieces marked "waltz ballad," blues ballad," "driving ballad," and so on. I am confident the reader will find these designations self-explanatory.

Duets and trios are annotated in the same manner as solos. Quartets and larger ensembles are designated only by voice part (a sextet would be listed as SATTBB, for example, without specific voice ranges), and choruses and company numbers (sung by some combination of chorus and principals) are given only a style or tempo label. Choruses are mixed voicing unless designated otherwise (men's, women's, or children's choruses). Any other pertinent or useful information is given at the end of a show's listings.

DEFINITIONS AND DESIGNATIONS

Only those vocal pieces which are excerptable have been included in this guide; no instrumental numbers have been annotated. A selection is deemed excerptable when it is able to be performed outside the context of a show. A piece where short phrases are passed between several characters without any real expository "aria" portion is therefore not listed as an excerptable solo song.

Musical numbers that are sung by a number of characters without any one character dominating, or that use most or all of the principal characters along with the chorus, are designated by the term "company." "Ensemble" numbers are for several principal characters without chorus. "Incidental" indicates that a character—in some cases the chorus—sings during the song but is not essential to its performance; taken out of context, a song may be performed by excluding these incidental portions, without harm to the musical fabric.

INDEXES

Indexes at the conclusion of the *Companion* are arranged by voice part, and within each voice part by three broad style categories:

Soprano	uptempo songs
	ballads
	character songs
Mezzo	uptempo songs
	ballads
	character songs

and so on, for tenors and then baritones. Duets, trios, and quartets are indexed alphabetically by title, with the voice type following (ST, SSA, TTBB, and so forth). Larger ensemble numbers are similarly listed, while choruses and company numbers are listed by type (women's, children's, men's, mixed) and then alphabetically by title. Within each of the above designations, titles of songs are always given in alphabetical order, followed by a page number referring the reader to the correct show, where the relevant information is located. Finally, there are alphabetical indexes to composers and lyricists. The appendix lists addresses for the publishers and agents of these shows.

Catalog

of Musicals

Ain't Misbehavin' (1978)

Music by Thomas "Fats" Waller, Hoagy Carmichael, others

Song title, Character (Voice)	Range	Song Style
Ain't misbehavin', company		ballad
'Tain't nobody's biz-ness if I do, company		uptempo
Lookin' good but feelin' bad, company		uptempo
Honeysuckle Rose, Ken (Bar), Nell (M)	d1-e♭2	ballad
Squeeze me, Amelia (M)	c1-f2	blues ballad
Handful of keys, Charlaine (S)	e♭-b♭2	ballad
I've got a feeling I'm falling, Nell	c1-e♭2	ballad
How ya baby, Andre (T)	c1-d2	swing uptempo
The jitterbug waltz, company	b♭-g2	waltz ballad
The ladies who sing with the band, Andre, Ken	e1-e2	uptempo
Yacht club swing, Charlaine	a♭-e♭2	swing ballad
When the nylons bloom again, Amelia, women	c1-d2	ballad
(Get some) Cash for your trash, Nell	a-e2	mod. uptempo
Off-time, women, then company		uptempo
The joint is jumpin', company		uptempo
Spreadin' rhythm around, company	d1-e2	ballad
Lounging at the Waldorf, Nell, Ken	c1-b2/c1-e♭2	ballad
The reefer song, Andre	c1-g2	blues ballad
Mean to me, Nell	c1-d2	ballad
Your feet's too big, Ken	c1-e♭2	hard jazz ballad
That ain't right, Amelia, Andre	g-a1	blues ballad
Keeping out of mischief now, Charlaine	a-c2	ballad
Find out what they like and how they like it, Nell	c1-d2	mod. uptempo
Fat and greasy, Andre, Ken	e1-e2	uptempo
(What did I do to be so) Black and blue, company		ballad
I'm gonna sit right down and write myself a letter, Ken	c1-e2	moving ballad
Two sleepy people, Ken, Amelia	c1-e2	ballad
I've got my fingers crossed, Charlaine	d1-f2	uptempo
I can't give you anything but love, Andre	e1-e2	mod. ballad
It's a sin to tell a lie, Andre, Nell	e1-e2	uptempo

Note: Ranges given are for entire songs, both parts included. The company sings backup on nearly every number, which is not indicated here.

Allegro (1947)

Music by Richard Rodgers   Lyrics by Oscar Hammerstein II

Song title, **Character (Voice)**	**Range**	**Song Style**
I know it can't happen again, Grandma (M)	b-b1	ballad
One foot, other foot, chorus		uptempo
A fellow needs a girl, Marjorie (S), Taylor (T) incidental	bb-f2	ballad
So far, Beulah (M)	c1-d2	ballad
You are never away, Joe (T), chorus incidental	B-g1	uptempo
What a lovely day for a wedding, chorus w/ soli	eb-f1	uptempo
It may be a good idea, Charlie (T)	d1-d2	uptempo
To have and to hold, company		uptempo
Money isn't everything, five women	SSMMM	waltz ballad
You are never away reprise, Joe	B-g1	uptempo
Ya-ta-ta, company		uptempo
The gentleman is a dope, Emily (M)	ab-bb1	mod. ballad
Allegro, company		uptempo
Come home, Marjorie	eb1-f2	ballad
Ya-ta-ta reprise, company		uptempo

Annie (1977)

Music by Charles Strouse   Lyrics by Martin Charnin

Song title, **Character (Voice)**	**Range**	**Song Style**
Maybe, Annie (girl S)	bb-d2	ballad
It's the hard-knock life, Orphan chorus		uptempo
Tomorrow, Annie	bb-eb2	ballad
Hooverville, chorus		mod. uptempo
Little girls, Miss Hannigan (M)	a-c2	mod. character
I think I'm gonna like it here, company		uptempo
N.Y.C., Warbucks (Bar), Grace (M), "Star to Be" (M) incidental	c-f1/c1-f2	ballad
Easy street, Rooster (T), Hannigan, Lily (S)	A-g1/a-f #2/a-f#2	mod. uptempo, blues ballad
You won't be an orphan for long, company		uptempo
Fully dressed, Bert (T), backup trio	e-f#1	mod. uptempo

Dressed children, ensemble		mod. uptempo
Cabinet "Tomorrow," Annie, Cabinet (male ensemble)		ballad
Cabinet end, Cabinet		ballad
Something was missing, Warbucks	c-f1	waltz ballad
I don't need anything but you, Annie, Warbucks	c#1-e2/c#-e1	uptempo
Servant's Annie, chorus		uptempo
Same effect on everyone (Maybe), Annie	bb-db2	ballad
A new deal for Christmas, company		uptempo

Note: See also *Annie Warbucks*.

Annie Get Your Gun (1946)
Music and Lyrics by Irving Berlin

Song title, Character (Voice)	Range	Song Style
Col. Buffalo Bill, Charlie (T), chorus	eb-f1	uptempo
I'm a bad, bad man, Frank (Bar), women's chorus	c-d1	mod. uptempo
Doin' what comes naturally, Annie (M), Kids and Wilson (both incidental)	c1-d2	character ballad
The girl that I marry, Frank	Bb-d1	waltz ballad
You can't get a man with a gun, Annie	bb-c2	character
There's no business like show business, Annie, Charlie, Buffalo Bill, Frank	bb-f2/men: Bb-f1	uptempo
They say it's wonderful, Frank, Annie	Bb-d1/bb-d2	ballad
Moonshine lullaby, Annie, three porters	ab-c2	blues ballad
I'll share it all with you, Tommy (T), Winnie (S)	d-eb1/d1-eb2	uptempo
There's no business like show business reprise, Annie	a-c#2	uptempo
My defences are down, Frank, chorus	c#-gb1	uptempo
I'm an Indian, too, Annie	bb-c#2	character
I got lost in his arms, Annie, chorus	bb-c2	mod. ballad
Why do you love I hope?, Tommy, Winnie	c-d1/c1-d2	mod. uptempo
I've got the sun in the morning, Annie, company	c1-c2	uptempo
The girl that I marry reprise, Frank	Bb-d1	ballad
Anything you can do, Annie, Frank	c1-g2/c-f1	character
There's no business like show business, company		uptempo
They say it's wonderful, company		ballad

Annie Warbucks (1993)

Music by Charles Strouse   Lyrics by Martin Charnin

Song title, Character (Voice)	Range	Song Style
Annie ain't just Annie anymore, company		uptempo
Above the law, Mrs. Doyle (M)	g#-b1	uptempo
Changes, Annie (girl S), Warbucks (Bar)	c1-d2/c-c1	ballad
The other woman, Orphan's chorus		narrative ballad
That's the kind of woman, Drake (Bar), Annie, chorus	c-f1/ab1-eb2	mod. uptempo
A younger man, Warbucks	Ab-e1	ballad
But you go on, Mrs. Kelly (M)	f#-b1	mod. uptempo
Above the law reprise, Mrs. Doyle, Mrs. Kelly	both a-d2	uptempo
I got me, Annie, Orphan's chorus	a-d2	moving ballad
Love, Ella (M)	f#-a1	gospel ballad
Somebody's gotta do somethin', company		uptempo
Leave it to the girls, Mrs. Doyle, Mrs. Kelly	both g-b1	uptempo
All dolled up, company		mostly uptempo
It would have been wonderful, Grace (S)	c1-eb2	moving ballad
When you smile, Warbucks, Annie	Bb-eb1/bb-eb2	mod. uptempo
I always knew, Annie	b-d2	mod. uptempo

Note: See also *Annie*.

Anyone Can Whistle (1964)

Music and Lyrics by Stephen Sondheim

Song title, Character (Voice)	Range	Song Style
Me and my town, Cora (M), chorus	a-eb2	character
Miracle song, Cora, chorus	f#-e2	uptempo
There won't be any trumpets, Fay (M)	g-c2	uptempo
Interrogation scene — Simple, Hapgood (Bar), George (Bar), ensemble	Bb-eb1/eb-eb1	character
A-1 march, chorus		uptempo
Come play wiz me, Fay, Hapgood	a-d2/A-e1	fast character
Anyone can whistle, Fay	g-b1	ballad
There's a parade in town, chorus		uptempo

Everybody says don't, Hapgood	G-e1	uptempo
I've got you to lean on, Cora (M),	MTTB/then	uptempo
Schub (T), Magruder (T), Cooley	Cora: a-d1	
(Bar)		
See what it gets you, Fay	g-c2	mod. ballad
Anyone can whistle reprise, Fay	a-d♭2	ballad
Cora's chase, Cora, chorus	a-e2	uptempo
Vocalise (S)	b1-d3	ad lib.
With so little to be sure of, Fay,	a-b1/B-e1	ballad
Hapgood		

Applause (1970)

Music by Charles Strouse   Lyrics by Lee Adams

Song title, Character (Voice)	Range	Song Style
Think how it's gonna be, Bill (T)	B-f1	ballad
But alive, Margo (M), men's chorus,	e-f#1	uptempo
Eve (M) incidental		
The best night of my life, Eve	g#-c#2	ballad
Who's that girl, Margo	e-a1	uptempo
Applause, Bonnie (M), chorus	g-c2	uptempo
Hurry back, Margo	a-f1	blues ballad
Fasten your seatbelts, company		uptempo
Welcome to the theater, Margo	d-f#1	angry uptempo
Good friends, Buzz (T), Karen (S),	c-g1/e♭-g2/c-f1	uptempo
Margo		
She's no longer a gypsy, Duane (T),		uptempo
Bonnie, chorus		
One of a kind, Bill, Margo	B♭-g1/c♭-a1	waltz uptempo
One Halloween, Eve	a♭-b♭1	ballad, then fast
Something greater, Margo, Bill	e♭1-g2	mod. ballad
incidental		
Bows: Applause, company		uptempo

The Apple Tree (1966)

Music by Jerry Bock   Lyrics by Sheldon Harnick

Song title, **Character (Voice)**	**Range**	**Song Style**
Part I		
Here in Eden, Eve (M)	a-a1	mod. uptempo
Feelings, Eve	b-e2	moving ballad
Eve, Adam (Bar)	d♭-d♭1	ballad
Friends, Eve	b♭-e2	ballad
Forbidden fruit, Snake (T)	d-g1	uptempo
Adam's reprise, Adam	d-e♭ 1	mod. ballad
Fish no. 1 and 2, Adam	d♭-d♭1	uptempo
Lullaby, Eve	b-b1	ballad
Fish no. 3, Adam	d♭-e♭1	uptempo
What makes me love him?, Eve	g#-c#2	ballad
Part II		
I'll tell you a truth, opening, Balladeer	c-e♭1	mod. uptempo
Make way, men's chorus		uptempo march
Ai, ai!, chorus		uptempo
Forbidden love, Barbara, Capt. Sanjar	b-e♭2/ b-e♭1	ballad
Razor teeth, Barbara, Balladeer	g-b♭1/d-g1	uptempo
I've got what you want, Barbara	a-c2	ballad
Tiger, tiger, Barbara	f-a1	driving uptempo
Make way – Canon, chorus		processional
Which door?, company		mod. uptempo
I'll tell you a truth, closing, Balladeer	c-f#1	slow, rubato
Part III		
Oh, to be a movie star, Ella	c1-d2	uptempo
Gorgeous, Ella	c1-d2	waltz uptempo
Who is she?, chorus, Ella solo at end		uptempo
I know, Ella, chorus	c1-e ♭2	uptempo
Wealth, Ella	c1-b	driving uptempo
Real, Flip, chorus	c-e♭	mod. uptempo
Oh, to be a movie star reprise, chorus		uptempo
Bows (pastiche of earlier music),		uptempo
company		

Note: Casting throughout show as follows:
    Eve = Barbara = Ella
    Adam = Capt. Sanjar = Flip
    Snake = Balladeer = Narrator

Assassins (1990)
Music and Lyrics by Stephen Sondheim

Song title, Character (Voice)	Range	Song Style
Opening, Proprietor (Bar), Booth (Bar), Assassins	G-f1/G-f1	character
The ballad of Booth, Balladeer (T), Booth	c#-g#1/F#-e1	narrative ballad
How I saved Roosevelt, Zangara (T), Bystanders	B-a1	uptempo
Gun song, Czolgosz (Bar), Booth, Guiteau (T), Moore (M)	G-c1/c-f#1/c-g1/a♭-e2	slow, funny
The ballad of Czolgosz, Balladeer, Crowd	d-g1	narrative ballad
Unworthy of your love, Hinckley (T), Fromme (M)	B-d#1/a-d#2	ballad
The ballad of Guiteau, Guiteau	A-g♭1	mod. ballad
Another national anthem, Balladeer, Assassins		mod. uptempo
Scene 16, Assassins		slow, dramatic
Everybody's got the right, company		mod. uptempo

Babes in Arms (1937)
Music by Richard Rodgers   Lyrics by Lorenz Hart

Song title, Character (Voice)	Range	Song Style
Babes in arms, Susie (S), chorus	d♭1-f2	uptempo
All at once, Susie, Val (T)	c1-e2/d-f1	ballad
I wish I were in love again, Terry (M), Gus (Bar)	d1-d2/d-d1	mod. ballad
Where or when, Jennifer (S), Val incidental	d1-g2	ballad
Way out West, Bunny (M)	c1-d2	character
Where or when reprise, Jennifer	c-f1	ballad
My funny valentine, Susie	c#1-e2	ballad
Finale act I, company		mod. uptempo
Imagine, Susie, Terry incidental	c1-e♭2	uptempo
You're nearer, Val, Susie	f-f1/d1-d2	uptempo
The lady is a tramp, Bunny	c#1-e2	fast character
My funny valentine reprise, Susie	a-b1	ballad
I wish I were in love again reprise, Terry, Gus	c1-d2/c-d1	mod. ballad

| *Johnny One Note*, Bunny | b♭-b♭1 (opt. e♭2) | fast character |
| *Finale act II: Johnny One Note*, company | | uptempo |

Babes in Toyland (1903)

Music by Victor Herbert   Lyrics by Glen MacDonough

Song title, **Character (Voice)**	**Range**	**Song Style**
Lemonade, company		mod. uptempo
Never mind, Bo Peep, company		fast character
Jane, Tom (T), women's chorus	c-e♭1 (opt. f1)	ballad
Before and after, Widow Piper (M), Barnaby (Bar)	b♭ - c2/B♭-c1	character
Floretta, Alan (Bar), women's chorus	G-e1	ballad
Mary, Mary, quite contrary, chorus		mod. uptempo
I'm in a hurry, Mary (S), chorus	d1-g2	character
Barney O'Flynn, chorus		mod. uptempo
Just a whisper away, Mary, Alan	d1-e2/d-e1	ballad
He won't be happy till he gets it, Roderigo (Bar), Gonzorgo (Bar)	both d-d1	character
Go to sleep, slumber deep, Fairy Queen (M), ensemble, Chorus of Fairies	d1-e2	ballad
Hand in hand, Jane (S), Alan	d1-f2/d-f1	ballad
Hail to Toyland, solo voice (S), chorus	d1-a2	uptempo
Toyland, Master Toymaker (Bar), chorus	c-e1	character
Just a toy!, Jill (S), chorus	c1-e2 (opt. a2)	character
Beatrice Barefacts, Mary, Marmaduke, (Bar), girl's trio	d1-e2/d-e1	character
March of the toys, Alan; chorus, Jane incidental	b♭-d1	character
Just a whisper away reprise, Mary, Alan	d1-e2/d-e1	ballad
Our castle in Spain, Jane, Tom	c1-d2/c-d1	ballad
Toyland reprise, company		uptempo

Baby (1984)

Music by David Shire   Lyrics by Richard Maltby, Jr.

Song title, Character (Voice)	Range	Song Style
We start today, company		uptempo
What could be better?, Danny (T), Lizzie (M)	f#-a1/a-e2	funny, uptempo
The Plaza song, Alan (Bar), Arlene (M)	c#-e1/d1-f2	mod. uptempo
Baby, baby, baby, Nick (Bar), Pam (M), company	c-f#1/g-f#2	mod. ballad
I want it all, Pam, Lizzie, Arlene	c1-e♭2/c1-e♭2/ b-e♭2	mod. ballad
At night she comes home to me, Nick, Danny	d-f1/d-g1	ballad, then uptempo
What could be better reprise, Danny, Lizzie	g-f1/c1-c2	uptempo
Fatherhood blues, men	TTBBB	uptempo march
Romance, Pam, Nick incidental	b-c#2	mod. ballad
I chose right, Danny	d-g1	moving ballad
We start today reprise, ensemble		uptempo
The story goes on, Lizzie	g-f2	quick ballad
The ladies singin' their song, women	SSAAA	jazzy uptempo
Patterns, Arlene	b♭-e♭2	ballad
Romance reprise, Nick, Pam	A-f#1/a1-f#2	ballad, then uptempo
Easier to love, Alan	c-e1	ballad
Two people in love, Danny, Lizzie	A-f#1 (opt. a1)/a-d2	uptempo
With you, Nick, Pam	A-e1/a-d2	ballad
And what if we had loved like that, Alan, Arlene	d-e1/d1-g2	mod. ballad
We start today reprise, company		uptempo
The story goes on, company		mod. uptempo

The Baker's Wife (1976)

Music and Lyrics by Stephen Schwartz

Song title, Character (Voice)	Range	Song Style
Chanson, Denise (M) (partially in French)	f#-b	waltz ballad
If it wasn't for you, company		mod. uptempo

Merci madame, Aimable (Bar), Genevieve (M)	A♭-e1/a♭-c2	mod. uptempo
Bread, company		uptempo
Gifts of love, Genevieve	g-e♭2	ballad
Proud lady, Dominique (T)	d-g1	uptempo
Look for the woman, company men		mod., funny
Serenade, Dominique, Denise, Phillippe (Bar), Aimable, Genevieve	MMTBB	mod. ballad
Meadowlark, Genevieve	e-e2	mod., narrative
Finale act I, company		uptempo
Chanson reprise, Denise (partially in French)	a-b1	mod. ballad
If it wasn't for you reprise, company		mod. uptempo
Any day now day, Aimable, company men	c-c1	uptempo
The world's luckiest man, company men		mod. uptempo
Feminine companionship, Marquis (T), company	c-f#1	funny, mod. uptempo
If I have to live alone, Aimable	B-c#1	ballad
Romance, company women		mod. ballad
Where is the warmth?, Genevieve	g#-b1	mod. uptempo
Finale act II, company		mod. uptempo

Barnum (1980)

Music by Cy Coleman   Lyrics by Michael Stewart

Song title, **Character (Voice)**	**Range**	**Song Style**
There is a sucker born ev'ry minute, Barnum (T)	c#-f1	uptempo
Thank God I'm old, Joice Heth (M)	g-c2	ballad
The colors of my life, Chairy (M), Barnum	g-b♭1/c-e♭1	ballad
One brick at a time, Chairy, chorus	g#-d2	uptempo
Museum song (Egress song), Barnum	d-e1	character
I like your style, Chairy, Barnum	c1-d2/c-d1	waltz ballad
Bigger isn't better, Tom Thumb (T)	d#-g1	fast character
Jenny Lind obbligato, Jenny Lind (S)	g1-c3	vocalise
Love makes such fools of us all, Jenny Lind	a-g2	ballad
Out there, Barnum	B♭-f1	uptempo
Come follow the band, company		uptempo

Love makes such fools . . . reprise, Jenny Lind	b♭-f2	ballad
Black and white, Blues Singer (S), Chairy, Barnum, chorus	e-a1/a-a1/e♭-f1	blues ballad
The colors of my life reprise, Chairy, Barnum	b-c#2/B-c#1	ballad
The prince of humbug, Barnum	c#-e1	uptempo
Join the circus, Barnum, Bailey (T), company	a♭1-f1/e-g♭1	uptempo

Bells Are Ringing (1956)

Music by Jule Styne   Lyrics by Betty Comden and Adolph Green

Song title, **Character (Voice)**	**Range**	**Song Style**
Bells are ringing, women's chorus		uptempo
It's a perfect relationship, Ella (M)	a♭-c♭2	ballad
Independent, Jeff (T), chorus	d-d1	mod. uptempo
It's a simple little system, Sandor (T), chorus	e♭-g1	fast character
Is it a crime, Ella	a♭-c2 (much spoken)	ballad
Better than a dream, Ella, Jeff	a-b1/e-d#1	ballad
Hello, hello there, chorus		uptempo
I met a girl, Jeff, chorus	c-g♭1	uptempo
Long before I knew you, Jeff, Ella	B-b♭1/b-c2	ballad
Mu-cha-cha, company		uptempo
Just in time, Jeff; Ella and chorus incidental	c#-d1	moving ballad
Drop that name, Ella, chorus	f#-b1	fast character
The party's over, Ella, chorus incidental	f#-b1	ballad
Salzburg, Sandor, Sue (S)	f-g♭1/e-g♭2	uptempo
The Midas touch, chorus		uptempo
Long before I knew you reprise, Jeff	c-c1	ballad
I'm going back, Ella	b♭-b♭1	ballad, then uptempo
He met a girl, chorus		uptempo

Best Foot Forward (1941)
Music and Lyrics by Hugh Martin and Ralph Blane

Song title, Character (Voice)	Range	Song Style
Don't see the night short, chorus		uptempo
Three men on a date, Dutch, Bud, Hunk	all d♭-f1	mod. uptempo
That's how I love the blues, Gale (M), Jack (Bar)	a-d2/A-c#1	blues ballad
The three "B"s, Minerva (M), Blind Date (M), Ethel (M)	b♭-e♭2/a♭-e♭2/b♭-g2	mod. uptempo
Ev'ry time, Helen (S)	c♭1-g♭2	mod. ballad
The guy who brought me can't send me, Gale; Dutch, Bud, Hunk incidental	b♭-c2	mod. uptempo
I know you by heart, Bud (Bar)	B-d#1	ballad
Shady ladybird, Helen	e♭1-f2	mod. uptempo
Buckle down, Winsocki, Greenie (T), chorus	d-g1	mod. march tempo
My first promise at my first prom, Ethel, chorus	e1-a2	waltz ballad
What do you think I am?, Minerva, Hunk (T)	a-e2/e-a1	uptempo
Just a little joint with a jukebox, Blind Date, chorus on encore	a-b1	mod. uptempo
Where do you travel, Jack, chorus incidental	B♭-c#	mod. uptempo, funny
Ev'ry time reprise, Gale	c1-e♭2	mod. ballad
Buckle down, Winsocki reprise, company		uptempo march

The Best Little Whorehouse in Texas (1977)
Music and Lyrics by Carol Hall

Song title, Character (Voice)	Range	Song Style
20 fans, company		moving ballad
A li'l ole bitty pissant country place, Mona (M), company	f-e2	mod. narrative ballad
Girl you're a woman, Mona, women's chorus	e-g#1	walking ballad
Texas has a whorehouse in it, Melvin (Bar), chorus	B♭-e♭1	fast character
Twenty-four hours of lovin', Jewel (M), chorus	e-g2	uptempo
Doatsey Mae, Doatsey Mae (M)	g-c2	ballad

The Aggie song, men's chorus		uptempo
The bus from Amarillo, Mona	e♭-b♭1	slow ballad
The sidestep, Governor (Bar), company	A-d1	fast character
No lies, Mona; Jewel, girls incidental	g-b1/c1-e2	mod. uptempo
Good old girl, Sheriff (Bar), men's chorus	G-f1	country ballad
Hard candy Christmas, women's chorus		hard blues ballad

Big River (1985)

Music and Lyrics by Roger Miller

Song title, **Character (Voice)**	**Range**	**Song Style**
Do ya wanna go to heaven, company		uptempo
The boys, male ensemble		uptempo
Waitin' for the light to shine, Huck (T)	d-e1	gospel ballad
Guv'ment, Pap (Bar)	B-f1	character ballad
Hand for the hog, Tom (T)	f-f1 (much spoken)	fast character
I, Huckleberry, me, Huck	c-f1	character ballad
Muddy water, Jim (Bar), Huck	b-f#1/b-a1	uptempo
The crossing, Mezzo solo	c1-c2	gospel ballad
River in the rain, Huck, Jim	A-g1/A-e1	ballad
When the sun goes down in the South, King (T), Duke (Bar), Huck, Jim	c-a1/e-a1/e-a1/B♭-g1	dixie ballad
The royal nonesuch, Duke, chorus	d-f1	fast character
World's apart, Jim, Huck	B-g1/B-b1 (falsetto)	ballad
Arkansas, Young Fool (T), King	d-e1/b-g1	hillbilly ballad
How blest we are, Daughter (S), chorus	g-c3	gospel ballad
You oughta be here with me, Mary Jane (M); Joanna (M), Susie (M) incidental	b-c#2/g-g1/g-g1	country ballad
How blest we are reprise, chorus		ballad
Leavin's not the only way to go, Huck, Mary Jane, Jim	b-b1/b1-b2/e-e1	ballad
Waitin' for the light to shine, Huck, chorus	a-f#	uptempo
Free at last, Jim, chorus	c-f1	gospel ballad
River in the rain reprise, Jim, Huck	both a-e1	ballad
Bows: Muddy water, Jim, Huck, chorus		uptempo

Bittersweet (1929)
Music and Lyrics by Noel Coward

Song title, Character (Voice)	Range	Song Style
That wonderful melody, chorus		ballad
The call of life, Lady Shayne (S), chorus	d1-a2	waltz ballad
If you could only come with me, Carl (T)	f#-g1	ballad
I'll see you again, Sarah (S), Carl	d♭1-a♭2/d♭-a♭1	mod. ballad
What is love, Sarah, chorus	e1-a2	waltz ballad
The last dance, chorus		uptempo
Eeny, meeny, mini, mo, Carl, company	B-g#1	uptempo
Life in the morning, chorus		uptempo
Ladies of the town, women's quartet	all c#1-e2	fast uptempo
If love were all, Manon (M)	b♭-f2 (opt. g2)	ballad
Dear little cafe, Sari (M), Carl	d1-g2/d1-g1	moving ballad
We wish to order wine, chorus		march tempo
Tokay, Capt. Schensi (Bar), chorus	c-e1	ballad
Bonne nuit, merci, Manon (in French)	e♭1-f2	mod. uptempo
Kiss me, Manon	c1-g2	waltz ballad
Ta-ra-ra-boom, chorus		uptempo
Alas, the time is past, women's sextet	SSMMMM	uptempo
Blasé boys are we, male quartet	all c-e1	mod. uptempo
Zigeuner ("Once upon a time"), Sari	c♭1-a♭2	waltz ballad

Added Song:

Evermore and a day, Sari, Carl	e♭1-g2/e♭-g1	ballad

The Boy Friend (1954)
Music and Lyrics by Sandy Wilson

Song title, Character (Voice)	Range	Song Style
Perfect young ladies, unison women's chorus		uptempo
The boy friend, Polly (S), chorus	c1-e2	mod. uptempo
Won't you Charleston?, Bobby (Bar), Maisie (M)	A-e1/a-e2	mod. uptempo
Fancy forgetting, Madame Dubonnet (S), Percival (T)	d1-g2/d-e1	uptempo

I could be happy with you, Tony (T), Polly	c-f1/c1-a2	ballad
The boy friend, ensemble		uptempo
Sur la plage, company		mod. uptempo
A room in Bloomsbury, Tony, Polly	c-g1/c1-g2	uptempo
It's nicer in Nice, Hortense (M), chorus	d1-g2	mod. ballad
The "you don't want to play with me" blues, Madame Dubonnet, Percival, women's chorus	c1-eb2/c#-d1	uptempo
Safety in numbers, Maisie, men's chorus	bb-f2	blues ballad
I could be happy with you, Tony, Polly	c-eb1/c1-eb2	uptempo
The riviera, chorus with incidental soli		ballad
It's never too late to fall in love, Lord Brockhurst (Bar), Dulcie (M)	d-eb1/d1-eb2	uptempo
Poor little Pierrette, Madame Dubonnet, Polly	bb-f1/g-bb2	mod. character
I could be happy with you reprise, chorus		uptempo

The Boys from Syracuse (1938)

Music by Richard Rodgers   Lyrics by Oscar Hammerstein II

***Song style*, Character (Voice)**	**Range**	**Song Style**
I had twins, company		uptempo
Dear old Syracuse, Antipholus of Syracuse (T)	A-f1	uptempo
What can you do with a man?, Luce (M), Dronio of Ephesus (T)	a-b1/d-e1	fast character
Falling in love with love, Adriana (S)	d1-ab2	ballad
The shortest day of the year, Antipholus of Ephesus (T), Adriana	d-f1/e1-f2	mod. uptempo
This can't be love, Antipholus of S., Luciana (S)	db-f1/db1-f2	mod. uptempo
This can't be love reprise, Luciana	d1-e2	mod. ballad
Ladies of the evening, chorus		uptempo
He and she, Luce, Dromio of S.	ab-eb2/Ab-eb1	ballad
You have cast your shadow on the sea, Antipholus of S., Luciana	eb-e1/c#1-e2	ballad
Come with me, Sergeant (T), men's chorus	c-g1	fast character

Big brother, Dromio of E. (T)	f-f1	ballad
Sing for your supper, Adriana, Luciana, Luce	c1-b♭2/b♭- g2/b♭-e♭2	uptempo
Oh, Diogenes, Courtesan (M), chorus	a-c2	uptempo
This can't be love, chorus		uptempo

Brigadoon (1947)

Music by Frederick Loewe   Lyrics by Alan Jay Lerner

Song title, Character (Voice)	Range	Song Style
Opening sequence: Prologue, Brigadoon, Vendor's calls, Down on MacConnachy Square, chorus, many soli		mostly uptempo
Waitin' for my dearie, Fiona (S), women's chorus	c1-a2	ballad
I'll go home with Bonnie Jean, Charlie (T), chorus	d-g1	uptempo
The heather on the hill, Tommy (high Bar)	b♭-f1	ballad
Rain scene, chorus		mod. uptempo
The love of my life, Meg (M)	g-c2	mod. ballad
Jeannie's packin' up, women's chorus		mod. uptempo
Come to me, bend to me, Charlie	d-g1	ballad
Almost like being in love, Tommy, Fiona	c-f#1/f1-a2	ballad, then uptempo
The chase, men's chorus, incidental soli		uptempo
There but for you go I, Tommy, Fiona	c-f1/spoken	ballad
My mother's wedding day, Meg, chorus	c1-f2	character
From this day on/Farewell, Tommy, Fiona, chorus	d-a1/d1-a2	mod. ballad
Finale: Reprises, company *Come to me, Heather on the hill, I'll go home, From this day on, Down on MacConnachy Square*		uptempo

Bye, Bye, Birdie (1960)

Music by Charles Strouse   Lyrics by Lee Adams

Song title, Character (Voice)	Range	Song Style
An English teacher, Rosie (M)	e#-a#1	uptempo
The telephone hour, chorus		fast character
How lovely to be a woman, Kim (S)	d#1-f#2	ballad
Put on a happy face, Albert (Bar)	B-e1	uptempo
A healthy, normal, American boy, company		moving ballad
Penn Station to Sweet Apple, chorus		ballad
One boy, Kim, Rosie, Two girls incidental	db1-ab2/ab-bb1	ballad
Honestly sincere, Conrad (T), chorus incidental	Ab-f1	swing ballad
Hymn for a Sunday evening, company		character
One last kiss, Conrad, chorus	Ab-f1	uptempo
What did I ever see in him, Rosie, Kim	both g-bb1	ballad
What did I ever see in him reprise, Rosie	g-bb1	ballad
A lot of livin' to do, Conrad, Kim, chorus	db-f1/e1-e2	uptempo
Kids, Mr. and Mrs. Macafee (Bar, M)	f-eb1/f1-eb2	uptempo
Baby, talk to me, Albert, male trio	f#-f#1	ballad
Kids reprise, chorus		uptempo
Spanish Rose, Rosie	g-c#2	uptempo
Rosie, Albert, Rosie	B-d1/a-bb1	ballad

Cabaret (1966)

Music by John Kander   Lyrics by Fred Ebb

Song title, Character (Voice)	Range	Song Style
Wilkommen, M.C. (T), girls	f#-e1	uptempo
Welcome to Berlin, M.C.	f#-e1	uptempo
So what, Fr. Schneider (M)	eb-bb1	character
Don't tell Mama, Sally (M), girls	a-a1	character ballad
Telephone dance, ensemble		mod. uptempo
Perfectly marvelous, Sally, Cliff (Bar)	f#-b1/c#-e1	uptempo
Two ladies, ensemble		mod. uptempo
It couldn't please me more, Fr. Schneider, Herr Schneider (Bar)	f#-a1/f#-g1	ballad

Tomorrow belongs to me, Tenor, chorus	a-a1	uptempo
Why should I wake up?, Cliff	B-e1 (opt. f1)	ballad
Sitting pretty, M.C., girls	e-g1	mod. uptempo
Married, Herr Schneider, Fr. Schneider	d-f1/a-a1	character ballad
Meeskite, Schultz (T), Sally incidental	f#-g1	character
Tomorrow belongs . . . reprise, Fr. Kost (M), company	a-b♭1	ballad
If you could see her, M.C.	d♭-a♭1	mod. ballad
What would you do?, Fr. Schneider	f-a1	ballad
Cabaret, Sally	e-c2	uptempo
Finale: Wilkommen reprise, company		uptempo

Note: 1987 Broadway version is different, including two new songs, "Don't Go" and "I Don't Care Much." Both "Meeskite" and "Why Should I Wake Up?" were dropped from that revised production.

La Cage aux Folles (1983)
Music and Lyrics by Jerry Herman

Song title, **Character (Voice)**	**Range**	**Song Style**
We are what we are, Les Cagelles (men's chorus)		mod. uptempo
A little more mascara, Albin (Bar), chorus incidental	B♭-d1	mod. ballad
With Anne on my arm, Jean-Michel (T)	A-g1	mod. uptempo
The promenade, company		fast waltz
Song on the sand, Georges (Bar)	A♭-e1	ballad
La cage aux folles, Albin, Les Cagelles	B♭-e1	uptempo
I am what I am, Albin	A-f1	hard ballad
Song on the sand reprise, Georges, Albin	both A-e1	ballad
Masculinity, George; Albin and chorus incidental	B-e1	mod. uptempo
Look over there, Georges	B-e1	waltz ballad
Cocktail counterpoint, Georges, Dindon (Bar), Mme. Dindon (M), Jacob (T)	A♭-b♭/B♭-e♭1/g1-a♭2/ B♭-a♭1	uptempo
The best of times, Albin, Jacqueline (M), chorus	c-e♭1/a#-b1	slow uptempo, builds
Look over there reprise, Jean-Michel, Georges incidental	d♭-d♭1	ballad
Grand finale: You on my arm, Georges, chorus	G#-d1	mod. uptempo

La cage aux folles, company		uptempo
The best of times, company		uptempo

Call Me Madam (1950)
Music and Lyrics by Irving Berlin

Song title, **Character (Voice)**	**Range**	**Song Style**
Mrs. Sally Adams, chorus		uptempo
The hostess with the mostes', Sally (M)	a-b1	fast character
The Washington Square dance, Sally, chorus	b♭-c2	uptempo
Lichtenburg, Cosmo (T), chorus	B♭-g1	mod. character
Marrying for love, Cosmo, Sally	G-c1/f-b♭1	ballad
The Ocarina, Princess Maria (S), chorus	c1-d2	uptempo
It's a lovely day today, Kenneth (T), Princess Maria, chorus	d-f1/d1-d2	light ballad
The best thing for you, Sally	a-c2	ballad
Something to dance about, Sally, chorus	b♭-c2	uptempo
Once upon a time, today, Kenneth	e-f1	narrative ballad
They like Ike, Wilkins, Brockbank, Gallagher (all T)	g-g1/g-f1/g-f1	fast character
(I wonder why) You're just in love, Kenneth, Sally	d-f#1/d1-c2	mod. ballad
The best thing for you reprise, Sally	b♭-b♭1	mod. uptempo
It's a lovely day today, Kenneth, Maria	c-d1/d1-d2	ballad
Mrs. Sally Adams, chorus		mod. uptempo
You're just in love reprise, Sally, chorus	a♭-c♭2	mod. uptempo

Camelot (1960)
Music by Frederick Loewe   Lyrics by Alan Jay Lerner

Song title, **Character (Voice)**	**Range**	**Song Style**
I wonder what the King is doing tonight, Arthur (Bar)	B♭-c1	uptempo
The simple joys of maidenhood, Guenevere (S)	c#1-d#2	mod. ballad
Camelot, Arthur	c-d1	uptempo
Follow me, women's chorus, incidental soli		mod. uptempo
C'est moi, Lancelot (T)	c-d1	uptempo

The lusty month of May, Guenevere, chorus	d1-a2	uptempo
How to handle a woman, Arthur	A-d1	ballad
The jousts, chorus		uptempo
Before I gaze at you again, Guenevere	c1-e♭2	ballad
Madrigal, Lancelot	c-b1	sprightly ballad
If ever I would leave you, Lancelot	A-d1	ballad
The seven deadly virtues, Modred (B)	c-d1	uptempo
What do the simple folk do? Guenevere, Arthur	c1-e♭2/B♭-e♭1	mod. character
The persuasion, Modred, Morgan (Bar)	spoken	character
I loved you once in silence, Guenevere	d♭-e♭2	ballad
Guenevere, Man (Bar), company	B-d1	mod. ballad
Camelot, company		uptempo

Can-Can (1953)
Music and Lyrics by Cole Porter

Song title, **Character (Voice)**	**Range**	**Song Style**
Maidens typical of France, women's chorus		uptempo
Never give anything away, Pistache (M), women's chorus	a-b1	ballad
C'est magnifique, Pistache, Aristide (T)	a-b♭1/g-e1	mod. ballad
Come along with me, Boris (Bar), Hilaire incidental	d-e1	uptempo
Live and let live, Pistache	g-b1	fast gavotte
I am in love, Aristide	d-f1	uptempo foxtrot
If you loved me truly, ensemble		uptempo
Monmart, chorus		uptempo
Allez-vous-en, Pistache	g-b1	ballad
Never, never be an artist, unison chorus, ensemble		uptempo
It's all right with me, Aristide	c#-e1	uptempo foxtrot
Every man is a stupid man, Pistache	b-a1	mod. ballad
I love Paris, Pistache, chorus	g-b1	ballad
C'est magnifique reprise, Aristide, Pistache	d-f1/d1-d2	ballad
Can-can, Pistache, chorus	b-b♭1	uptempo
Monmart reprise, company		uptempo

Candide (1956)

Music by Leonard Bernstein   Lyrics by Richard Wilbur

Song title, **Character (Voice)**	**Range**	**Song Style**
The best of all possible worlds, company		uptempo
Oh, happy we, Candide (T), Cunegonde (S)	d-a1/d1-a2	uptempo, light
It must be so, Candide	d-e1	recit. folk ballad
Lisbon sequence, company, incidental soli		mod. uptempo
It must be me, Candide	d-e1	recit. ballad
Glitter and be gay, Cunegonde	eb1-eb3	fast showpiece
You were dead, you know, Candide, Cunegonde	e-e1/e1-g#2	character ballad
Pilgrim's processions, company		moderate
My love, Governor (T)	db-bb1	character march
I am easily assimilated, Old Lady (M), Cunegonde and chorus incidental	d1-e2	character, tango
Finale act I: Farewell, Cunegonde, Candide, Old Lady, Governor	SATB	uptempo
Quiet, Cunegonde, Old Lady, Governor incidental	d1-f2/g-f2	mod. ballad
Eldorado, Candide, chorus	db-f#1	ballad
Bon voyage, Governor, chorus	c-bb1	character
Venice gambling scene, Croupie (incidental Bar), company		funny, uptempo
What's the use?, company		character
The Venice gavotte, ensemble		character
Make our garden grow, company		mod. uptempo

Added Song:

| *Dear boy*, Pangloss (Bar) | B-f#1 | character ballad |

Carnival (1961)

Music and Lyrics by Bob Merrill

Song title, **Character (Voice)**	**Range**	**Song Style**
Direct from Vienna, company		mod. uptempo
Very nice man, Lili (S)	bb-f#2	ballad
I've got to find a reason, Paul (T)	Bb-f1	mod. ballad

Mira, Lili	c-f1	uptempo
Sword, rose, and cape, Marco (Bar), Roustabouts (male ensemble)	e♭-e♭1	uptempo
Humming, Rosalie (M), Schelgel (Bar)	b♭-c2/B♭-b♭	uptempo
Yes, my heart, Lili, men's chorus	d♭1-f#2	uptempo
Everybody likes you, Paul	B♭-e♭1	mod. ballad
Magic magic, Rosalie, Marco; Lili incidental	d1-d2/d-d1	uptempo
Golden delicious ("Love makes the world go 'round"), Lili; Carrot Top and Horrible Henry incidental	c1-d2	moving ballad
Love makes the world go 'round reprise, Lili, company	b♭-b♭2	mod. waltz
Her face, Paul	B-e♭1	easy ballad
Cirque de Paris, Jacquot (T), Roustabouts	c-c1	uptempo
I hate him, Lili, Paul	c1-b2/A-c1	fast, then mod.
Paris reprise, chorus		uptempo
Always, always you, Marco, Rosalie	A-d1/a-f2	mod. ballad
Always you reprise, Rosalie	g-b♭1	mod. ballad
She's my love, Paul	B♭-e♭1	ballad

Carousel (1945)

Music by Richard Rodgers   Lyrics by Oscar Hammerstein II

Song title, **Character (Voice)**	**Range**	**Song Style**
Mister Snow, Carrie (S), Julie incidental	d1-g2	mod. uptempo
If I loved you, Billy (T), Julie (S)	B♭-g♭1/c1-g♭2	ballad
June is bustin' out all over, chorus		uptempo
Mister Snow reprise, Carrie, Mr. Snow (T)	d1-d1/f#-a1	mod. uptempo
When the children are asleep, Mr. Snow, Carrie	e♭-a1/c#1-f2	ballad
Blow high, blow low, Jigger (Bar), Billy, men's chorus	both d-b	character
Soliloquy, Billy	B-g1	epic ballad
June is bustin' out all over reprise, chorus		uptempo
A real nice clambake, company		mod. uptempo
Geraniums in the winder/Stonecutters cut it on stone, Mr. Snow, Jigger, chorus	d-f#1/c-b	mod. ballad
What's the use of wond'rin', Julie, girl's chorus	c1-f2	moving ballad

You'll never walk alone, Nettie (M), Julie incidental	c1-g2	ballad
The highest judge of all, Billy	d-g1	mod. uptempo
If I loved you reprise, Billy	db-gb1	ballad
Graduation scene, chorus		mod. ballad

The Cat and the Fiddle (1932)

Music by Jerome Kern   Lyrics by Otto Harbach

Song title, Character (Voice)	Range	Song Style
La jeune fille, Mme. Abajour (M)	b-c2	ballad
The night was made for love, Pompineau (T)	eb-ab1	ballad
She didn't say "yes," Pompineau, Shirley (M)	e-f#1/e1-f#2	moving ballad
La jeune fille reprise, Mme. Abajour	eb-ab1	ballad
The love parade, Pompineau, Maizie (M), chorus	e-f1/e1-b1	moving ballad
Victor's studio, Constance (S), Odette (M), Victor (T)	c1-a2/c1-g2/c-g1	ballad
The breeze kissed your hair, Victor, Odette	c-g1/e1-f2	ballad
Try to forget, Shirley	a-e2	ballad
Tableau scene, Commère (M), Coupère (Bar)	b-f#2/G-e1	character
Try to forget, company		uptempo
The crystal candelabra, Pompineau	d-g1	uptempo
She didn't say "yes" reprise, Shirley, Pompineau	e1-g2/c-f1	ballad
A new love is old, Victor	db-gb1	ballad
One moment alone, Shirley, Victor, offstage chorus	ab1-ab2/ab-gb1	ballad
Phantasy, offstage chorus		mod. uptempo
Hh! Cha! Cha!, Shirley	eb1-eb2	mod. uptempo
She didn't say "yes" reprise, company		uptempo

Celebration (1969)

Music by Harvey Schmidt   Lyrics by Tom Jones

Song title, Character (Voice)	Range	Song Style
Celebration, Potemkin (Bar), chorus	A♭-d♭1	uptempo
Orphan in the storm, Orphan (boy), chorus	b♭-e♭2	ballad
Survive, Potemkin, incidental chorus	c♭-e♭1	ballad
Somebody, Angel (M), chorus	f-c2	moving ballad
Bored, Rich (Bar)	G-e♭1	mod. fast, funny
My garden, Orphan, chorus	g-f2	moving ballad
Where did it go?, Rich, chorus*	B-e1	jazzy ballad
Love song, company		ballad
I'm glad to see you got what you want, Orphan, Angel	b♭-d2/b♭-f2	ballad
It's you who makes me young, Rich, incidental chorus	G-c1	uptempo, Latin beat
Not my problem, Potemkin, chorus*	B♭-f1	angry ballad
Fifty million years ago, Orphan	e♭-f2	uptempo
Beautician ballet, Rich, women's chorus	G-c1	fast character
Under the tree, Angel, women's chorus	b-e2	ballad
Winter and summer, chorus		driving ballad
Celebration reprise, company		uptempo

*Chorus may be omitted for solo.

Chess (1988)

Music by Benny Andersson and Björn Ulvaeus   Lyrics by Tim Rice

Song title, Character (Voice)	Range	Song Style
Press conference, Florence (M), company	d1-d2	uptempo
Where I want to be, Anatoly (T)	e-f1	driving ballad
How many women, Florence, Freddie (T)	e-c#1/a-g1	uptempo
Merchandiser's song, ensemble		mod. uptempo
U.S. versus U.S.S.R., Molokov (B), chorus	G-c#1	mod. ballad
A model of decorum and tranquility, Molokov, Florence, Arbiter (Bar), Anatoly	c#-d1/f-f2/F-e♭1/F-e	uptempo

You want to lose your only friend?, Florence, Freddie	e-g1/G-a1	driving ballad
Someone else's story, Florence	f-c2	ballad
One night in Bangkok, Freddie, chorus	d-a1 (much spoken)	uptempo
Terrace duet, Florence, Anatoly	a-e2/A-f1	ballad
So you got what you want, Freddie, Florence	e-c♭2, b-b1	uptempo
Nobody's side, Florence, backup chorus	e-e2	ballad
Anthem, Anatoly	c#-g1	ballad
Hungarian folk song, company		anthem ballad
Heaven help my heart, Florence	a♭-b♭1	ballad
No contest, Freddie, Walter (T)	f-a1/g-a1	mod. uptempo
You and I, Anatoly, Florence, Svetlana (M)	c-g1/g-c2/e#-b1	mod. ballad
A whole new board game, Freddie	e1-a1	driving uptempo
Let's work together, Walter, Molokov	c-d1 (d2 falsetto)/D-d1	recit. like, mod. uptempo
I know him so well, Florence, Svetlana	f-d2/f-c2	ballad
Pity the child, Freddie	B♭-d♭2	slow ballad
Lullaby (Apukad eros kezen), Gregor (B), Florence	A-d1/b-g1	ballad
Endgame, Anatoly, Freddie, company	c-a1/c#-g#1	uptempo
You and I reprise, Anatoly, Florence	A-f1/g-d1	moving ballad
Anthem reprise, Florence	a♭-d♭1	ballad

Chicago (1975)

Music by John Kander   Lyrics by Fred Ebb

Song title, **Character (Voice)**	**Range**	**Song Style**
All that jazz, Velma (M), company	g#-c2	mod., hard jazz
Funny honey, Roxie (M)	f-b♭1	blues ballad
Cell block tango, six girls	SSAAAA	mod. ballad
When you're good to mama, Matron (S)	f#1-a2	uptempo, torch
All I care about, Billy (T), women	c-f#1	mod. ballad
A little bit of good, Mary Sunshine (S)	b♭-b♭2	uptempo
We both reached for the gun, company		uptempo
Roxie, Roxie, men	g♭-d2	mod. fast jazz
I can't do it alone, Velma	f#-c2	mod. uptempo
My own best friend, Roxie, women	g-f2	mod. ballad
I know a girl, Velma	e-a1	mod. uptempo
Me and my baby, Roxie, men incidental	b♭-c2	uptempo
Mister Cellophane, Amos (T)	c#-f#1	ragtime ballad

When Velma takes the stand, Velma, men	spoken	hard, jazz uptempo
Razzle dazzle, Billy, company	d-f1	mod. uptempo
Class, Velma, Matron	f#-b♭1/f#-g1	moving ballad
Nowadays, Roxie	f#-g1	ballad
Nowadays reprise, Velma, Roxie	both f#-a♭1	ballad

Chorus Line (1975)

Music by Marvin Hamlisch   Lyrics by Edward Kleban

Song title, **Character (Voice)**	**Range**	**Song Style**
Opening: I hope I get it, company		uptempo
I can do that, Mike (T)	g-a♭1	mod., narrative
". . . and . . .," company		moderate
At the ballet, Sheila (M), Bebe (M), Maggie (S)	e-d2/a-c2/a-e2	waltz ballad
Sing!, Kristine (M), Al (T)	spoken/g-g#1	character, funny
Hello, twelve, company		uptempo
Nothing, Morales (M)	g-b1	mod., narrative
Mother, company		narrative
Gimme the ball, Richie (T)	c#-g1	uptempo
Dance: ten; looks:three, Val (M)	b♭-d♭2	mod., funny
The music and the mirror, Cassie (M)	b-d2	moving ballad
One, company		mod. uptempo
What I did for love, Morales, company	b♭-b♭1	ballad
One reprise, company		uptempo

Cinderella (1957)*

Music by Richard Rodgers   Lyrics by Oscar Hammerstein II

Song title, **Character (Voice)**	**Range**	**Song Style**
The Prince is giving a ball, chorus, many soli		uptempo
In my own little corner, Cinderella (S)	d1-d2	moving ballad
Your majesties, King (T), Queen (M), others incidental	c-f1/b-b1	character
Boys and girls like you and me, Queen, King	b-e2/B-e1	ballad
In my own little corner reprise, Cinderella	d1-d2	ballad

Impossible, Godmother (M), Cinderella incidental	d1-d2	uptempo
It's possible, Godmother, Cinderella	both d♭1-d♭2	uptempo
Ten minutes ago, Prince (T), Cinderella	c-d1/c#1-d2	waltz ballad
Stepsister's lament, Joy (M), Portia (M)	both c1-d2	fast character
Waltz for a ball, chorus		waltz ballad
Do I love you because you're beautiful, Prince, Cinderella	e-e1/d1-d2	ballad
When you're driving through the moonlight, Cinderella	b-b1	uptempo
A lovely night, Cinderella, Stepsisters	d1-d2/SS: c1-d2	ballad
Do I love you . . . reprise, Prince, Queen incidental	c-e1	ballad
The wedding, "Do I love you," company		ballad

*Originally written for CBS Television.

City of Angels (1989)

Music by Cy Coleman   Lyrics by David Zippel

Song title, **Character (Voice)**	**Range**	**Song Style**
Prologue, Angel City Four*	SATB*	uptempo
Double talk, Stine (T)	B#-g#1	mod. uptempo
What you don't know about women, Gabby (M), Oolie (M)	both g-f2	hard, jazzy ballad
Stay with me, Jimmy Powers (T), Angel City Four	g-g1	40s ballad
You gotta look out for yourself, Jimmy, Angel City Four	c-e1	uptempo
The Buddy system, Buddy (Bar)	c-d1	fast, jazzy waltz
With every breath I take, Bobbi (M)	e-d♭1	blues ballad
The tennis song, Alaura (M), Stone (Bar)	g-e2/G-d1	funny ballad
Everybody's gotta be somewhere, Stone, Angel City Four	c-b1	uptempo
Lost and found, Mallory (M)	g#-c#2	jazz ballad
All you have to do is wait, Muñoz (high Bar), TBB trio incidental	d-f#1	mod. Latin ballad
You're nothing without me, Stine, Stone	d-g1/d-e1	mod. uptempo
Stay with me, nos. 2-3, Jimmy, Angel City Four	c-g1	ballad
You can always count on me, Ooolie/ Donna	a-d♭2	mod. funny ballad

It needs work, Gabby	a♭-c2	mod. ballad
With every breath I take reprise, Bobbi, Stone	d#-c2/G#-e1	ballad
Funny, Stine	B♭-f1	hard ballad
I'm nothing without you, Stine, Stone, company	d-g1/d-e1	mod. uptempo

*Angel City Four, inclusive ranges for all numbers:
  S = a-a2
  A = a-d2
  T = d#-b1
  B = G-g#1

The following singing roles are double-cast:
  Gabby/Bobbi
  Oolie/Donna
  Carla/Alaura

Closer than Ever (1989)

Music by David Shire   Lyrics by Richard Maltby, Jr.

Song title, Character (Voice)	Range	Song Style
Doors, company		uptempo
She loves me not, Woman 1 (S), Man 1 (T), Man 2 (Bar)	b♭-f2/c-a1/c-e2	uptempo
You wanna be my friend, Woman 2 (M), Man 2 incidental	e♭1-d♭2	uptempo
What am I doin', Man 1	c-a2	driving ballad
The bear, the tiger, the hamster, and the mole, Woman 1	a♭-d♭2	mod. uptempo, funny
Like a baby, Man 2, Woman 1, 2	B♭-d1/b♭-e♭2/ b♭-c2	ballad
Miss Byrd, Woman 2	f-d♭2 (with scatted g2)	character
The sound of muzak, company		uptempo
One of the good guys, Man 1	c-f1	ballad
There's nothing like it, company		uptempo
Life story, Woman 1	b♭-c2	ballad
Next time/I wouldn't go back, company, Man 3		mod. uptempo
Three friends, Woman 1, Woman 2, Man 1	a#-f#2/a#- c#2/a#-a1	uptempo
Fandango, Woman 1, Man 2	c1-d2/c-d1	funny, uptempo
There, Woman 2, Man 3 (Bar)	a-c#2/A-f1	whimsical, slow

Patterns, Woman 1	b♭-e♭2	ballad
Another wedding song, Woman 2, Man 2	b♭-c2/b-c1	mod. ballad
If I sing, Man 2	A-e♭1	ballad
Back on base, Woman 2	g-c#2	swing ballad
The march of time, company		uptempo
Fathers of fathers, Man 1, 2, 3	e-g1/others e-f1	moving ballad
It's never that easy/I've been here before, Woman 1, 2	b-g2/g-d1	ballad
Closer than ever, company + Man 3		moving ballad

Added Song:

I'll get up tomorrow morning, Man 2	B♭-e1	uptempo, patter song

Company (1970)
Music and Lyrics by Stephen Sondheim

Song title, Character (Voice)	Range	Song Style
Company, Robert (T), ensemble	c-a♭1	uptempo
Little things, Joanne (M), chorus	c#-f#1	character
Sorry-Grateful, Harry (Bar), David (Bar), Larry (Bar)	all d-e1	ballad
You could drive a person crazy, April (S), Marta (M), Kathy (M)	e1-a2/e1-e2/e1-e2	uptempo
Have I got a girl for you, ensemble		mod. uptempo
Someone is waiting, Robert	c#-f#1	ballad
Another hundred people, Marta, chorus incidental	c1-e♭2	uptempo
Getting married today, Amy (S), chorus with soli	a-a1	uptempo, patter song
Side by side by side/What would we do without you?, company		uptempo
Poor baby, ensemble (various duets)		mod. uptempo
Barcelona, Robert, April	B♭-e♭1/b♭-e♭2	mod. ballad
The ladies who lunch, Joanne	e-a1	character ballad
Being alive, Robert	f-g#1	uptempo
Company reprise, company		uptempo

Note: The show was revived in 1995 with one added song, not available for this annotation.

Countess Maritza (1926)

Music by Emmerich Kálmán   Lyrics by Harry B. Smith

Song title, Character (Voice)	Range	Song Style
Dear home of mine, Tassilo (T), Nepomuk (Bar)	c#-g#1/B-e1	ballad
Hola! Follow me, Lazlo (T), chorus	d-a1	uptempo
Live while you live, Manya (S)	d1-g2	uptempo
Call of love, Tassilo, Manya	c-d1/c1-g2	ballad
In the days gone by, Tassilo, Stefan (T)	c#-f#1/e-a1 (opt. b1)	ballad
Make up your mind, Zingo (T), chorus	d-f#1	fast character
The music thrills me, Maritza (S), chorus	a#-b2	uptempo
Sister mine, Tassilo, Liza (S)	d-f1/g1-bb2	waltz ballad
Sons of Mars, unison men's chorus		uptempo march
The one I'm looking for, Maritza, Zupan (Bar), chorus	d1-e2/B-f#1	mod. uptempo
Don't tempt me!, Tassilo, Manya	d-bb1/c1-a2	recit.-like, fast
Love has found my heart, Maritza	e1-b2	waltz ballad
I'll keep on dreaming, Liza, Zupan	c1-g2/c-g1	ballad
Love is just a flash of light, Maritza, Tassilo	d1-a2 (opt. b2)/d-g1	mod. ballad
Play gypsies! Dance gypsies!, company		uptempo
Joy of life, Manya, Zupan, Zingo	mostly unsion, d-e1	uptempo

The Cradle Will Rock (1938)

Music and Lyrics by Marc Blitzstein

Song title, Character (Voice)	Range	Song Style
I'm checkin home now, Moll (M), Gent (Bar), Dick (Bar)	f#-d2/Bb-a/c-b	ballad, then faster
Nightcourt scene, company		uptempo
Dear Mrs. Mister, Mrs. Mister (M), Rev. Salvation (Bar)	bb-eb2/e-e1	mod. uptempo
Croon, Junior (T), Sister (M)	B-d1/b-d2	mod. ballad
I have called you here, Mr. Mister (Bar), Editor Daily (T)	c-d1/d-a1	uptempo
Let's do something/Honolulu, Mr. Mister, Editor Daily, Junior, Sister	c-c1/c-f1/c-f1/c-d2	uptempo

Drugstore scene, Steve (T), Druggist (Bar), Bugs (Bar)	b-c1/c-d1/ spoken	mod. uptempo
I wonder if anyone could be in love as we, Gus (T), Sadie (M)	B-f#1/b-e♭2	ballad
Don't let me keep you, Dauber (Bar), Yasha (Bar)	both G#-e♭1	mod. uptempo
And we love art for art's sake, Dauber, Yasha	both e-d1	uptempo
Maybe you wonder, Moll	f#-c2	mod. ballad
Makin' a speech, Larry (Bar)	spoken	mod. ballad
The cradle will rock, Larry	A#-d#1	mod. uptempo
Hello doctor, Ella (M)	a-b♭1	mod. character
Listen, here's a story, Ella	f-b♭1	mod. uptempo
The cradle will rock reprise, chorus		mod. uptempo

Crazy for You (1991)

Music and Lyrics by George and Ira Gershwin

Song title, Character (Voice)	**Range**	**Song Style**
K-ra-zy for you, Bobby (T)	B♭-e♭1	uptempo
I can't be bothered now, Bobby, girls	d-f1	mod. uptempo
Bidin' my time, Cowboy Trio: Sam (Bar), Mingo (T), Moose (B)	d-d1/d-g1/c-b	mod. ballad
Things are looking up, Bobby	c-d1	mod. uptempo
Could you use me?, Bobby, Polly (M)	A-e♭1/a-d2	uptempo
Shall we dance, Bobby	d♭-f♭1	uptempo
Girls enter Nevada/Bronco busters, chorus		uptempo
Someone to watch over me, Polly	a♭-b♭1	moving ballad
Slap that bass, company		mod. uptempo
Embraceable you, Polly	a-b1	moving ballad
Tonight's the night, chorus		uptempo
I got rhythm, Polly, company	b-d♭	uptempo
The real American folksong, Cowboy Trio, chorus	c-a1/c-f1/A-d1	mod. uptempo
What causes that?, Bobby, Zangler (Bar)	both c-f1	funny, mod. uptempo
Naughty baby, Irene (M), Lank (Bar) incidental, male quartet	a♭-b♭1	mod. uptempo
Stiff upper lip, company		mod. uptempo
They can't take that away from me, Bobby	B♭-e♭1	swing ballad

But not for me, Polly	b♭-c2	ballad
Nice work if you can get it, Bobby, girls	d-d1	swing uptempo
Bidin' my time reprise, Cowboy Trio*	c1-g1/d-d1/c-c1	uptempo
Who could ask for anything more, company		uptempo
Embraceable you, company		ballad

*Sung in French.

Dames at Sea (1968)

Music by Jim Wise   Lyrics by George Haimsohn and Robin Miller

Song title, **Character (Voice)**	**Range**	**Song Style**
Wall Street, Mona (M)	b-b1	uptempo
It's you, Ruby (M), Dick (T)	d1-e♭2/d-e♭1	jazzy ballad
Broadway baby, Dick	d-a1	uptempo
That Mister Man of mine, Mona, chorus	g-d#2	mod. uptempo
Choo choo honeymoon, Joan (M), Lucky (Bar)	b♭-e♭2/B♭-e♭1	mod. ballad
The sailor of my dreams, Ruby	a♭-d♭2	mod. ballad
Singapore Sue, company		uptempo
Good times reprise, company		uptempo
Dames at sea, Lucky, Dick, Captain (T), girls trio	all d-f#1 (one to g1)	uptempo
Beguine, Mona, Captain	d1-f#2/e-a♭1	beguine ballad
Raining in my heart, Ruby, chorus	a♭-d#2	mod. ballad
Something about you, Ruby, Dick	d1-d2/d-e1 (opt. f1)	mod. ballad
Echo waltz, Ruby, Joan, Mona, men offstage	women all d♭1-f2	waltz ballad
Star tar, Ruby, chorus	g#-c#2	uptempo march
Simple wedding, company		mod. uptempo

Damn Yankees (1955)

Music and Lyrics by Richard Adler and Jerry Ross

Song title, **Character (Voice)**	**Range**	**Song Style**
Six months out of every year, Meg (M), chorus	g-b1	fast uptempo
Goodbye old girl, Young Joe (T)	d-f1	ballad
Heart, Van Buren (T), ball players (men's chorus)	e♭-f1	uptempo

Heart reprise, ball players		uptempo
Shoeless Joe from Hannibal, Mo.,	b♭-d♭2	uptempo
Gloria (M), men		
A man doesn't know, Joe	B♭-d1	ballad
A little brains, a little talent, Lola (M)	g-a1	fast, character
A man doesn't know reprise, Joe, Meg	c-f1/g-c2	ballad
Whatever Lola wants, Lola gets, Lola	f-c♭2	sleazy character
Heart reprise, ensemble		uptempo
Who's got the pain, Lola, Eddie (Bar)	B♭-b1/b♭-b2	jazz uptempo
The game, ball players		uptempo
Near to you, Joe, Meg	c-f♭1/a-c2	ballad
Those were the good old days,	B-d1	mod. character
Applegate (Bar)		
Two lost souls, Lola, Joe	both d-d1	ballad
A man doesn't know reprise, Meg, Joe	a♭-f2/f-f1	ballad
Bows: Heart, company		uptempo

Dear World (1973)

Music and Lyrics by Jerry Herman

Song title, Character (Voice)	Range	Song Style
Thru the bottom of the glass, Countess (M)	e-b1	mod. ballad
Just a little bit more, President (Bar), Prospector (Bar), Lawyer (T)	A♭-e♭1/c♭-f♭1/c-f♭1	uptempo
Each tomorrow morning, Countess, chorus	f-b♭1	ballad
I don't want to know, Countess	g#-a♭1	waltz ballad
I've never said I love you, Nina (M)	a-e♭2	mod. ballad
Pretty garbage, Sewerman (Bar), Countess, Constance (M), Gabrielle (M)	A-e/a-e2 b-e2/a♭-e	moderate
Ugly garbage, Sewerman, Constance, Gabrielle, chorus	men B-e1/b-e2	moderate
One person, Countess, chorus	f-b♭1	mod. uptempo
The spring of next year, President, Prospector, Lawyer	G-d1/B♭-e♭1/ B♭-g1	waltz ballad
Memory, Constance	b-e♭2	character ballad
Dickie, Gabrielle, Countess incidental	g-e2	mod. uptempo
Voices, Constance	e1-e2	mod. uptempo
Thought, Countess	g-d1	ballad
Tea party trio, Countess, Constance, Gabrielle	g-d1/e-e1/g-c2	mod. uptempo

And I was beautiful, Countess	g-d2	ballad
Dear world, Julian (Bar), company	E-a (half-spoken)	mod. uptempo
Spring of next year reprise, chorus		ballad
Kiss her now, Countess	f#-a1	ballad
Dear world reprise, company		mod. uptempo

The Desert Song (1926)
Music by Sigmund Romberg
Lyrics by Otto Harbach, Oscar Hammerstein II, Frank Mandel

Song title, **Character (Voice)**	**Range**	**Song Style**
High on a hill, Sid (T), men's chorus	e-a1	anthem ballad
The riff song, Red Shadow (T), Sid, men's chorus	d-g1/f-a1	ballad
Margot, Paul (Bar), men's chorus	e-e1	ballad
Why did we marry soldiers?, women's chorus		character
Oh girls, here are cavaliers, Margot (S), chorus	f1-c3	uptempo
Romance, Margot, women's chorus incidental	d1-bb2	waltz ballad
Then you will know, Margot, Pierre (T), chorus	f-b2/c-eb1	ballad
I want a kiss, ensemble, chorus		mod. uptempo
It, Susan (M), Bennie (Bar)	d1-d2/d-d1	fast uptempo
The desert song, Margot, Red Shadow	eb1-bb2/db-gb1	waltz ballad
Oh, lucky Paul, tell us all, company		uptempo
My little castagnette, Clementina (S), women's chorus	e1-a2	uptempo
Song of the brass key, Clementina, women's chorus, Ali (Bar) incidental	e1-g2	character ballad
One good boy gone wrong, Clementina, Bennie	d1-f#2/d-g1	uptempo
Eastern and western love, ensemble, men's chorus		ballad
The sabre song, Margot, Red Shadow incidental	d1-bb2 (opt. c3)	ballad
All hail to the general, women's chorus		uptempo
It reprise, Bennie	eb-f1	uptempo

Destry Rides Again (1959)

Music and Lyrics by Harold Rome

Song title, **Character (Voice)**	**Range**	**Song Style**
Don't take me back to Bottleneck, chorus		uptempo
Ladies, Frenchy (M), women's chorus	a-d♭2	uptempo
Hoop-de-dingle, Wash (T), chorus	B-f1	fast character
Tomorrow morning, Destry (Bar)	d♭-d♭1 (spoken)	character ballad
Ballad of a gun, Destry, Wash incidental	c-e♭1 (much spoken)	fast character
I know your mind, Frenchy	e-a1	tango torch song
I hate him, Frenchy	g#-c#2	uptempo, angry
Paradise alley, chorus		mod. uptempo
Anyone would love you, Destry, Frenchy	B♭-c1/g-a1	ballad
Once knew a fella, Destry, men's chorus	B-e1	uptempo
Every once in a while, men's chorus		uptempo
Fair warning, Frenchy	f-c2	uptempo
Ballad of a gun reprise, chorus		uptempo
Are you ready, Gyp Watson?, ensemble, chorus		funereal ballad
Not guilty, men's chorus		slow, character
Only time will tell, Destry, chorus	c-d1 (much spoken)	narrative ballad
Respectability, Rose (M), women's chorus	g-b♭1	ballad
Ring on the finger, Frenchy, women's chorus	f-b♭1	ballad
Once knew a fella reprise, Frenchy, Destry	a-b1/A-d1	uptempo
I say hello, Frenchy	f-a1	ballad
Dirge, chorus		slow
Ballad of a gun reprise, company		uptempo

Do I Hear a Waltz? (1965)

Music by Richard Rodgers   Lyrics by Stephen Sondheim

Song title, **Character (Voice)**	**Range**	**Song Style**
Someone woke up, Leona (M)	a-b1	uptempo
This week, Americans, Fioria (M)	a-b♭1	character

Song title	Range	Song Style
What do we do? We fly!, ensemble		character
Someone woke up reprise, Leona	a-b1	uptempo
Someone like you, DiRossi (T)	e-f1	ballad
Bargaining, DiRossi	B♭-e3 (falsetto)	fast character
Here we are again, Leona, company	g#-b1	mod. ballad
Thinking, DiRossi, Leona	B-d#1/a-d#2	uptempo
Here we are again reprise, ensemble		ballad
No understand, Eddie (T), Fioria, Giovanna (S)	c#-d1/c#1-d2/a-e2	character
Take the moment, DiRossi	d-a♭1	moving ballad
Moon in my window, Jennifer (M), Fioria, Leona	b-d2/g-a1/g#-a	ballad
We're gonna be all right, Eddie, Jennifer	a-d1/a1-d2	uptempo
Do I hear a waltz?, Leona	a-d♭2	waltz ballad
Stay, DiRossi	a-d♭2	ballad
Perfectly lovely couple, ensemble		uptempo
Take the moment reprise, DiRossi	d-f1	ballad
Last week, Americans, Leona	a-a1	character
Thank you so much, Leona, DiRossi	b♭-d2/d-d1	ballad

Do, Re, Mi (1960)

Music by Jule Styne   Lyrics by Betty Comden and Adolph Green

Song title, Character (Voice)	Range	Song Style
Waiting, Kay (M)	b♭-d♭1	moving ballad
All you need is a quarter, chorus		uptempo
Take a job, Hubie (T), Kay	G-g1/c-e2	moving ballad
All you need is a quarter reprise, chorus		fast–Lindy Hop
It's legitimate, Hubie, Fatso (T), chorus	c#-f#1/e-a2	walking ballad
I know about love, Wheeler (Bar)	B-g1	ballad
Cry like the wind, Tilde (S)	b-b2	ballad
Ambition, Hubie, Tilde incidental	c#-e1/d1-a2	uptempo
Fireworks, Wheeler, Tilde	B-g1/b-g2	uptempo
What's new at the zoo?, Tilde, women's chorus	b-c#2	jazzy ballad
Asking for you, Wheeler	c-f1	ballad
The late, late show, Hubie	c-d1	uptempo
Adventure, Hubie, Kay	c#-c#1/g#-d♭2	uptempo
Make someone happy, Wheeler, Tilde	c-f1/b-f2	ballad
Who is Mr. Big?, ensemble, chorus		mod. uptempo
He's a V.I.P., chorus		mod. uptempo
All of my life, Hubie	c-e1	forceful ballad
Make someone happy reprise, company		uptempo

Dreamgirls (1981)

Music by Henry Krieger   Lyrics by Tom Eyen

Song title, **Character (Voice)**	**Range**	**Song Style**
I'm looking for something, baby, company		uptempo
Tiny Joe Dixon, Tiny Joe (T)	g-g1	blues ballad
Move (you're steppin' on my heart), Effie (M), Lorrell (S), Deena (M) (Dreamettes)	bb-f2/d1-eb2 d1-db2	uptempo
Fake your way to the top, Jimmy (T), Dreamettes, offstage chorus	f-ab1	mod. uptempo
Cadillac car, Curtis (T), ensemble	f-g1	uptempo
Steppin' to the bad side, company		mod. jazz ballad
Party party, ensemble		uptempo
Baby, baby, Jimmy, Dreamettes	f-g1	ballad
Family, ensemble		ballad
Dreamgirls, Deena, Effie, Lorell	a-e2/c#1-e2/c#1-a2	uptempo
Reporters, ensemble		uptempo
Heavy, Deena, Effie, Lorrell, Curtis incidental	d1-c2/eb1-eb2/e1-bb2	narrative ballad
It's all over, ensemble		uptempo
(And I'm telling you) I'm not going, Effie, ensemble	eb1-f2	uptempo
Opening act II, company		mod. uptempo
You are my dream, Curtis, ensemble	c-e1	mod. ballad
Ain't no party, Jimmy, Lorrell, TTBBB ensemble	g-ab1/bb-gb2	mod. swing ballad
I mean you no harm/Rap, ensemble	SSAAT (mostly spoken)	slow, then faster
I miss you old friend, ensemble, Les Styles (4 girls)		uptempo
One night only, Effie, chorus	ab-db2	mod. ballad
One night only — disco, company		uptempo
Chicago, ensemble		mod. uptempo
Hard to say goodbye (my love), ensemble		moving ballad

Eubie (1979)

Music by Eubie Blake, arranged by Danny Holgate
Lyrics by Noble Sissle, Andy Razaf, Johnny Brandon,
F. E. Miller, and Jim Europe

Song title, **Character (Voice)**	**Range**	**Song Style**
Shuffle along, company		mod. uptempo
In honeysuckle time, Man 1 (Bar), backup chorus	B-e1	ballad
I'm just wild about Harry, Women 1, 3, 4, 5 (M)	all b♭-d2	mod. uptempo
Daddy, Woman 3	g-e2	blues ballad
I'm a great big baby, Man 5 (T)	d-a1	moderate, jazzy
My handyman ain't handy anymore, Woman 6 (M)	b♭-c2	funny ballad
Low down blues, Man 4 (T)	d-f1	blues ballad
Gee, I wish I had someone to rock me in the cradle of love, Woman 4, Man 4	c1-g2/f-a♭1	moving ballad
I'm just simply full of jazz, company		uptempo
High steppin' days, company		mod. uptempo
Dixie moon, Man 3 (T), chorus	d-f1	mod. uptempo
Weary, Woman 2 (S), chorus	d1-a2	blues ballad
Roll Jordan, company		gospel uptempo
Memories of you, Woman 4	g-e♭2	ballad
If you've never been vamped by a brownskin, you've never been vamped at all, Woman 5, company	b♭-b♭2	funny uptempo
You got to git the gittin' while the gittin's good, Man 2 (Bar)	e-e1	mod. uptempo
Oriental blues, Man 5 (Bar), women	d-e1	blues ballad
I'm craving for that kind of love, Woman 3	b♭-a♭1	ballad
Hot feet, company		uptempo
Goodnight Angeline, company		slow
Finale: I'm just wild about Harry, company		uptempo

Evita (1979)

Music by Andrew Lloyd Webber   Lyrics by Tim Rice

Song title, Character (Voice)	Range	Song Style
Requiem, chorus		ballad
Oh, what a circus, Che (T), Eva (S)	B-a♭1/a♭1-d2	uptempo, angry
On this night of 1000 stars, Magaldi (T), Eva, Che, chorus	d-g1/g-f2/d-a1	Latin ballad
Buenos Aires, Eva	e-f1	jazzy uptempo
Goodnight and thank you, Che, Eva, Magaldi, chorus	g-c2/e1-e♭2/d#-c2	mod. uptempo
The art of the possible, Evita, Generals (male ensemble)	d1-f2	character
Another suitcase, Mistress (M), Eva incidental	a-e1	ballad
Peron's last home, company		narrative mod.
A new Argentina, chorus		mod. dramatic
Balcony/Casa Rosada, Eva, Peron (B)	a♭-e♭2/B♭-g♭1	dramatic ballad
High flying adored, Che, Eva	B-g1/a-e2	moving ballad
Rainbow high, Eva, chorus	e-g2	uptempo
Rainbow tour, company		uptempo
And the money kept rolling in, Che, chorus	A-g1	driving uptempo
Santa Evita, children, chorus		ballad
Waltz for Eva and Che, Eva, Che	a♭-f2/d-g1	character
She's a diamond, Peron, Generals	A-f1	recit., character
Dice are rolling, Peron, Eva	A-f1/a-e♭2	recitative
Eva's final broadcast, Eva, Che incidental	a♭-d♭2	ballad
Montage, ensemble		moderate

Note: Music is continuous with little spoken dialogue.

Falsettoland (1990)

Music and Lyrics by William Finn

Song title, Character (Voice)	Range	Song Style
Falsettoland/It's about time, company		mod. ballad
Year of the child, company		mod. uptempo
Miracle of Judaism, Jason (boy S)	g-b♭1	mod. ballad
The baseball game, company		uptempo, funny
A day in Falsettoland, Mendel (Bar), company	e♭-f♭1	mod. ballad

Racquetball I, Whizzer (T), Marvin (T), Jason, company	B#-f#1/B#-g1/d♭-d♭1	uptempo, recit.-like
The argument, Marvin, Trina (M), Jason, Mendel	all mostly e-e1	uptempo, angry
Everyone hates his parents, Mendel, company	B-d2	character ballad
What more can I say, Marvin	d♭-d1	ballad
Something bad is happening, Charlotte (M), Cordelia (M)	b♭-e2/b♭-e♭2	mod. ballad
Racquetball II, Marvin, Whizzer	both B#-f#	uptempo recit.
Trina's song, Trina	g-d2	mod. ballad
Days like this, company		mod. uptempo
Cancelling the bar mitzvah, Trina, Marvin, Jason	a-d2/A-d1/d1-c2	mod. ballad
Unlikely lovers, Marvin, Whizzer, Cordelia, Charlotte	B-f1/c#-g1/b-e2/b-c#2	ballad
Miracle reprise, Jason	g-b1	ballad
You gotta die sometime, Whizzer	c-g1	mod., angry
The bar mitzvah, company		uptempo
What would I do, Marvin, Whizzer	A-f#1/e-f#1	ballad

Note: See also *March of the Falsettos*, the second half of *Falsettos* (1992) of which *Falsettoland* is the first half.

Fanny (1954)

Music and Lyrics by Harold Rome

Song title, Character (Voice)	Range	Song Style
Restless heart, Marius (T), men's chorus	e♭-b♭1	uptempo
Never too late for love, Panisse (Bar), women's chorus	c#-d1	mostly ballad
Restless heart duet, Marius, Fanny (S)	whistles/e1-e2	uptempo
Why be afraid to dance?, Cesar (Bar), company	d-d1	uptempo
Hakim's cellar, chorus		mod. uptempo
Welcome home, Cesar	A-b	uptempo
I like you, Marius, Cesar	d-g♭1/e♭-c♭1	ballad
I have to tell you, Fanny	e1-a2	uptempo
Fanny, Marius	d-g1	moving ballad
Love motif, chorus		uptempo
The sailing, chorus		ballad
Oysters, cockles and mussels, chorus		mod. uptempo
Panisse and son, Panisse	c#-e1	uptempo

Wedding scene, ensemble		moderate
Finale I: Easter morning, chorus		uptempo
Happy birthday scene, ensemble, chorus		uptempo
To my wife, Panisse	c-d1	ballad
The thought of you, Marius, Fanny	e-a1/a1-f2	uptempo
Love is a very light thing, Cesar	A-b♭	waltz ballad
Fanny reprise, Cesar, Marius, Fanny incidental	B♭-e♭1/A-b♭	ballad
Be kind to your parents, Fanny, Cesar	a-e2/A-c1	fast character
Scene: Front of curtain, chorus		anthem ballad
Welcome home reprise, Panisse, Cesar	both A-a	ballad

The Fantastiks (1960)

Music by Harvey Schmidt   Lyrics by Tom Jones

Song title, Character (Voice)	**Range**	**Song Style**
Try to remember, El Gallo (Bar); Luisa, Matt incidental	A-c1	ballad
Much more, Luisa (S)	b-f2	moving ballad
Metaphor, Luisa, Matt (T)	b-g2/d-d1	moving ballad
Never say no, Huck, Bill (both Bar)	both c-e1	fast character
It depends on what you pay, El Gallo, Huck, Bill	A-g1/both d-f#1	character, evil
Soon it's gonna rain, Luisa, Matt	d1-f2/c-f1	ballad
Happy ending, company		uptempo
This plum is too ripe, company		uptempo
I can see it, Matt, El Gallo	B-f1/A-d1	moving ballad
Plant a radish, Bill, Huck	B-f1/d-f1	mod. character
'Round and 'round, Luisa, El Gallo	c#1-b♭2/A♭-e♭1	waltz ballad
They were you, Matt, Luisa	B-d1/b-d2	ballad
Try to remember reprise, El Gallo, company	A-c1	ballad

Fiddler on the Roof (1964)

Music by Jerry Bock   Lyrics by Sheldon Harnick

Song title, Character (Voice)	**Range**	**Song Style**
Tradition, company		mod. uptempo
Matchmaker, Hodel (M), Chava (M), Tzeitel (S)	b-c2/b-c2/b-d2	uptempo waltz

If I were a rich man, Tevye (B)	c-f1	mod. character
Sabbath prayer, Tevye, Golde (M), chorus	d-c1/d1-c2	anthem ballad
To life, ensemble		uptempo
Tevye's monologue, Tevye	A♭-e♭1	ballad, recit.
Miracle of miracles, Motel (T)	e-f#1	uptempo
The dream, chorus		moderate
Sunrise, sunset, Golde, Tevye	c1-a♭1/f-d♭1	ballad
Now I have everything, Perchik (Bar), Hodel	B-e1/b-e2	ballad
Do you love me?, Tevye, Golde	c-d1/c1-d2	mod. ballad
The rumor, chorus		mod. uptempo
Far from the home I love, Hodel	c1-e♭2	ballad
Chava sequence, Tevye, company	c-c1	uptempo
Anatevka, company		mod. ballad

Finian's Rainbow (1947)

Music by Burton Lane   Lyrics by E. Y. Harburg

Song title, Character (Voice)	Range	Song Style
This time of the year, company		uptempo
How are things in Glocca Morra?, Sharon (S)	a♭-d♭2	ballad
Woody's entrance, chorus		uptempo
Look to the rainbow, Sharon, chorus incidental	a♭-d♭2	ballad
Old devil moon, Woody (T), Sharon	d-e1/b♭-d♭2	jazzy ballad
How are things . . . reprise, Sharon	b♭-d♭2	ballad
Something sort of grandish, Og (T), Sharon	B-f#1/c1-e2	uptempo
If this isn't love, Woody, Sharon, Finian, chorus incidental	c-f1	uptempo
Something sort of grandish reprise, Og	c#-f#1	uptempo
Necessity, women's chorus		uptempo
That great come-and-get-it day, company		uptempo
When the idle poor become the idle rich, Sharon, chorus	b-a2	uptempo
Old devil moon reprise, Woody, Sharon incidental	d-f1	jazzy ballad
The begat, Senator (T) and TBB trio	TTBB	uptempo
That great come-and-get-it day reprise, company		uptempo

Fiorello! (1959)

Music by Jerry Bock   Lyrics by Sheldon Harnick

Song title, Character (Voice)	Range	Song Style
On the side of the angels, Neil (Bar), then Morris (Bar)	both d♭-e1	uptempo
Angels counter, ensemble		uptempo
Politics and poker, Card Players (male ensemble)	TTTBBBB	uptempo waltz
Unfair no. 1, women's chorus, Dora		uptempo
Unfair, Fiorello version, Fiorello (T), women	d-e1	driving uptempo
Marie's law, Marie (M), Morris	a#-e#2/A#-c#1	mod. ballad
The name's LaGuardia, Fiorello, chorus	c-g1	uptempo
The bum won, Card Players	TTTBBBB	mod. ballad
I love a cop, Dora (M)	c1-e2	fast character
I love a cop reprise, ensemble		uptempo
Till tomorrow, Thea (S), Marie, Morris, chorus	both c1-e2/c-e1	waltz ballad
Home again, chorus		uptempo
When did I fall in love, Thea	d1-g2	fast, then slower
Gentleman Jimmy, Mitzi (M)	g-c2	mod. uptempo
Gentelman Jim reprise, chorus		mod. uptempo
Little tin box, Card Players	TTTBBBB	soft shoe
The very next man, Marie	g#-d1	moving ballad
Politics and poker reprise, men's chorus		uptempo waltz
Very next man reprise, Marie	a-d2	ballad
The name's LaGuardia reprise, company		uptempo
Home again, company		uptempo

The Firefly (1912)

Music by Rudolph Friml   Lyrics by Otto Harbach

Song title, Character (Voice)	Range	Song Style
A trip to Bermuda, company		uptempo
He says yes, she says no, Geraldine (S), Jack (T), chorus	g1-a2/g-c2	uptempo
Call me uncle, Thurston (Bar), chorus	A-d1	fast character
Love is like a firefly, Nina (S)	c1-a♭2	character ballad
Something, Jenkins (T), Suzette (M)	c#-f#1/f#1-g#2	ballad
Gianna mia, Nina	d#1-b2	ballad

I've found it at last, company		uptempo
In sapphire seas, Sybil (M), ensemble	d1-c3 (opt. g3)	slow ballad
Tommy Atkins, Nina	d1-g2	fast character
Sympathy, Geraldine, Thurston	e1-f#2/e-f#1	character, funny
A woman's smile, Jack	c-a1	ballad
De trop, Jenkins, Suzette, Pietro (T)	c-f1/e1-a2/e-a1	character
We're gonna make a man of you, quintet	STTTB	uptempo, funny
The beautiful ship from Toyland, Franz (Bar), men's chorus	B♭-f1	mod. character
When a maid comes knocking at your heart, Nina	c1-a2	mod. ballad
Waltz, chorus		waltz ballad
An American Beauty rose, Thurston, chorus	c-f1	ballad
The latest thing from Paris, Pietro, Suzette	d-g1/d1-g2	uptempo
The dawn of love, Nina	d1-b♭2	ballad

Five Guys Named Moe (1991)
Music by Louis Jordan, arranged by Clarke Peters

Song title, **Character (Voice)**	**Range**	**Song Style**
Early in the morning (prerecorded Bar)	c#-f1	uptempo
Five guys named Moe, company	TTTBB	swing ballad
Brother, beware, Big Moe (Bar)	a♭-g♭1	uptempo
I like them fat like that, Little Moe (T)	(spoken)	mod. ballad
Messy Bessy, No Moe (T)	e♭-g1	mod. shuffle
Pettin' and pokin'/Life is so peculiar, company	all e♭-g1	uptempo
I know what I've got/Azure-te, Nomax (Bar), Four-eyed Moe (high Bar)	B♭-g1/e♭-g1	mod. uptempo
Knock me a kiss, company		moderate, jazzy
Safe, sane, and single, company		uptempo
Push ka pi she pie, No Moe (Bar), Eat Moe (T), Four-eyed Moe	all g-d1	uptempo
Saturday night fish fry, Nomax, company	f-b♭1	uptempo
What's the use of gettin' sober/If I had any sense I'd go back home, Big Moe	c-e1	ballad

Dad gum your hide boy, Little Moe, No Moe, company	both g-d1	uptempo
The cabaret, Big Moe, company	b♭-f1	uptempo
There ain't nobody here but us chickens, Four-eyed Moe, No Moe	c-e1/spoken	mod. uptempo
Don't let the sun catch you crying, Eat Moe	B♭-b♭1 (falsetto)	moving ballad
Choo choo ch'boogie, Little Moe, company	f-f1	mod. uptempo
Look out sister, Four-eyed Moe	a♭-f1 (some spoken)	uptempo
Is you is—medley, company		ballad
Five guys named Moe reprise, company		swing ballad

Florodora (1900)

Music by Leslie Stuart

Lyrics by Owen Hall

Song title, Character (Voice)	Range	Song Style
Opening chorus, chorus		uptempo
The credit's due to me, men's ensemble		mod. character
The silver star of love, Dolores (S)	d♭1-a♭2	ballad
Somebody, Dolores, Abercoed (Bar)	a-a2/c#-e1	lilting ballad
Huzzah the master comes, chorus		uptempo
Come and see our island, company		uptempo
When I leave town, Lady Holyrood (M)	d1-e2	fast character
Galloping, Angela (M), Donegal (T)	c#1-f#2/B-f#1	uptempo
I want to marry a man, I do, Lady Holyrood, Tweedlepunch (Bar), Gilfain (Bar)	b-d2/c-c1/B-c1	fast character
The fellow who might, Angela, chorus incidental	c1-e2	narrative ballad
Phrenology, Gilfain (T), chorus	B-f1	fast character
When an interesting person, Lady Holyrood, Donegal, Angela	f1-f2/d-f1/a-f2	uptempo, funny
The shade of the palm, Abercoed	B♭-e♭1	narrative ballad
Hey, hey, alack aday!, company		mod. ballad
Come lads and lasses, company		uptempo
Tact, Lady Holyrood	c#1-d2	character
The millionaire, Gilfain	c-e1	uptempo
Tell me, pretty maiden, chorus		mod. ballad
I've an inkling, Lady Holyrood	c1-e2	character ballad
And the nations will declare you, company		anthem ballad

Supplementary Numbers:

The queen of the Philippine Islands, Dolores	b-a2	narrative ballad
We get up at 8 a.m., Valleda (S), Leandro	e1-e2/e-e1	character
(Bar)	d-f1	fast character
I want to be a military man, Donegal, chorus	b♭-g2	ballad
He loves, he loves me not, Dolores	c1-d2	narrative ballad
Willie was a day boy, Angela	b-g2/B-g1	ballad
When we are on the stage, Dolores, Tweedlepunch	b♭-g2	waltz ballad
The island of love, Dolores, chorus		

Flower Drum Song (1958)

Music by Richard Rodgers   Lyrics by Oscar Hammerstein II

Song title, Character (Voice)	Range	Song Style
You are beautiful, Madam Liang (M), Wang Ta (T)	f-c2/e-g1	ballad
A hundred million miracles, ensemble		uptempo
I enjoy being a girl, Linda (M)	a-c#2	uptempo
I am going to like it here, Mei Li (M)	b♭-b♭1	ballad
Like a god, Wang Ta, Mei Li incidental	c#-g1	uptempo
Chop suey, Madam Liang, chorus incidental	g-c2	uptempo
Don't marry me, Sammy Fong (Bar), Mei Li*	d-e1/d1-c2	uptempo
Grant Avenue, Linda, chorus incidental	a-c2	uptempo
Love, look away, Helen (S)	d1-f2	ballad
Fan tan Fanny, Solo S	d1-d2	jazzy uptempo
Gliding through my memoree, Franki (Bar), girls	B-d1	fast character
Love look away reprise, Helen	f1-a♭2	ballad
The other generation, Madam Liang, Wang Ta	both e♭-c♭1	uptempo
You are beautiful reprise, Wang Ta	f-g1	ballad
Sunday, Linda, Sammy	d1-c2/d-e1	mod. ballad
Don't marry me reprise, Sammy	d-e1	ballad
The other generation reprise, company		uptempo
A hundred million miracles reprise, company		uptempo

*Mostly a solo for Sammy.

Follies (1971)
Music and Lyrics by Stephen Sondheim

Song title, Character (Voice)	Range	Song Style
Beautiful girls, Roscoe (T), company	e-a1	mod. ballad
Don't look at me, Sally (M), Ben (Bar)	a-b1/c#-c#1	ballad
Waiting for the girls upstairs, ensemble		ballad
Rain on the roof, The Whitmans (M, Bar)*	B♭-d1/b♭-d2	ballad
Ah, Paris!, Solange (S)*	c#1-g2	uptempo
Broadway baby, Hattie (M)*	a-b1	jazzy ballad
The road you didn't take, Ben	a-e1	ballad
In Buddy's eyes, Sally	f#-d2	uptempo
Who's that woman, Stella (M), women's chorus	f#-f#2	mostly uptempo
I'm still here, Carlotta (M)	e♭-c2	blues ballad
Too many mornings, Ben, Sally	c-e1/c1-g#2	ballad
The right girl, Buddy (Bar)	c-f1	uptempo
One more kiss, Heidi (S), Young Heidi (girl S)	d-g2/e1-a♭2	waltz ballad
Could I leave you, Phyllis (M)	f#-b1	uptempo waltz
"LOVELAND"		
Loveland, company		uptempo
You're gonna love tomorrow, Young Ben (T), Young Phyllis (S)	c#-f#1/c#1-e♭2	ballad
Love will see us through, Young Buddy (T), Young Sally (S)	d-f1/e♭1-g♭2	ballad
The god-why-don't-you-love-me blues, Buddy; Rita (S), Suzanne (M) incidental	d-f1 (opt. a1)	uptempo blues
Losing my mind, Sally	f-b1	ballad
The story of Lucy and Jessie, Phyllis, chorus incidental	g-b1	narrative mod.
Live, laugh, love, Ben, company	c-f1	mod. uptempo

* "Rain on the Roof," "Ah, Paris!," and "Broadway Baby" are combined at end into a trio quodlibet.

Forever Plaid (1993)
(Many different compsers and lyricists from 1950s)

Song title, **Character (Voice)**	**Song Style**
Three coins in a fountain, Frankie	ballad
Gotta be this or that, Sparky	uptempo
Moments to remember, Jinx	ballad
Crazy 'bout ya baby, Frankie	mod., moving
No not much, Jinx	mod. uptempo
Perfidia, Sparky	mod., funny
Cry, Jinx	mod. ballad
Sixteen tons, Smudge	character ballad
The chain gang, Frankie*	ballad
The catering drill, company	mostly uptempo
The bride cuts the cake	
The tarantella	
Anniversary waltz	
Little town of Bethlehem	
Hava naghelah	
Rock my soul	
She loves you	
A tribute to Mr. C.	
Dream along with me, Jinx	ballad
Sing to me, Mr. C., Sparky	waltz ballad
Catch a falling star, Sparky	moving ballad
The Plaids go calypso	fast, Caribbean
Day-O, Jinx	feel
Kingston market, Jinx	
Jamaica farewell, Smudge, Sparky	
Mathilda, Frankie	
Heart and soul, Frankie	swing ballad
Lady of Spain, Jinx	cafe ballad
Scotland the brave, company	anthem ballad
Shangri-la/Rags to riches, Smudge	mod. uptempo
Love is a many splendered thing, company	ballad

* "Sixteen Tons" and "Chain Gang" then combined in a quodlibet.

Vocal ranges of the singers:
    Jinx (T)   B-e2 (falsetto)
    Frankie (T)   B-a1
    Sparky (Bar) A-f#1 (g#1 in falsetto)
    Smudge (B)   F-f#1 (d2 in falsetto)

The Fortune Teller (1898)

Music by Victor Herbert   Lyrics by Harry B. Smith

Song title, Character (Voice)	Range	Song Style
Introduction, Fresco (Bar), women's chorus	G-e1	uptempo
Always do as people say you should, Irma (S)	e1-b♭2	mod. ballad
Hungaria's hussars, Ladislas (T), men's chorus	e-a1	fast character
Ho! Ye townsmen, Sandor (Bar)	G-d1	slow character
Romany life, Musette (S), ensemble incidental	a-b♭2 (opt. d3)	uptempo
I, a bride, company		uptempo
Chime for the bride so fair, chorus		uptempo
Signor Mons. Muldoni, Fresco (Bar), chorus	B-d1	narrative ballad
Serenades of all nations, company		various
Slumber on my little gypsy sweetheart, Sandor	A-c1	ballad
Only in the play, Pompon (M), Ladislas	d1-g2/d-g1	waltz ballad
Eljen! Eljen! Vivat!, company		uptempo
Gypsy Jan, Sandor, chorus	G-e♭1	narrative ballad
The power of the human eye, Boris (Bar), Count (B)	f-e♭1/E♭-e♭	ballad
The lily and the nightingale, Musette	d1-c3	ballad
Thro' the forest wild and free, company		uptempo

Forty-Second Street (1980)

Music by Harry Warren   Lyrics by Al Dubin

Song title, Character (Voice)	Range	Song Style
Young and healthy, Billy (T), Peggy (M)	B♭-g1/b♭-c#2	mod. uptempo
Shadow waltz, Dorothy (M), women's chorus	g-a1	waltz ballad
Go into your dance, Maggie (M), Andy (Bar), women	b♭-b♭1/d-d♭1	mod. uptempo
You're getting to be a habit with me, Dorothy	a-a1	ballad
Dames, Billy, women's chorus	d-a1	mod. uptempo
I know now, Dorothy, Billy, chorus	e♭-a♭1/d-g1	easy ballad

We're in the money, company		mod. uptempo
Forty-second Street, Dorothy	bb-g1	mod. uptempo
There's a sunny side to every situation, company		mod. uptempo
Lullaby of Broadway, company		swing ballad
About a quarter to nine, Dorothy, Peggy	both eb-bb1	ballad
Shuffle off to Buffalo, women's chorus		shuffle ballad
Forty-second Street, Peggy	b-b1	mod. uptempo
Bows:Dames/Lullaby of Broadway, company		uptempo

Funny Girl (1964)

Music by Jule Styne   Lyrics by Bob Merrill

Song title, **Character (Voice)**	**Range**	**Song Style**
If a girl isn't pretty, company		uptempo
I'm the greatest star, Fanny (M)	g-c2	uptempo
Cornet man, Fanny, chorus	a#-f2	jazz ballad
Who taught her everything?, Mrs. Brice (M), Eddie (T)	ab-e2/eb-f1	soft shoe ballad
His love makes me beautiful, Solo T, women	d-bb1	slow, then uptempo
I want to be seen with you tonight, Nick (Bar), Fanny	ab-eb1/ab-f2	ballad
Henry Street, chorus		waltz ballad
People, Fanny	ab-db1	ballad
You are woman, I am man, Nick, Fanny	a#-e1/b#-c#2	ballad
Don't rain on my parade, Fanny	e-b1	uptempo
Sadie, Sadie, Fanny, chorus	a-eb2	ballad
Find yourself a man, Mrs. Brice, Mrs. Strakosh (M), Eddie	women bb-d2/ Bb-d1	waltz ballad
Rat-tat-tat-tat, Eddie, chorus	d-f#1	uptempo march
Private Schwartz, Fanny, chorus	b-d#2	character
Who are you now?, Fanny	bb-db1	ballad
Don't rain on my parade reprise, Nick	d-d1	uptempo
The music that makes me dance, Fanny	g#-e2	ballad
Don't rain . . . finale, Fanny	e-b1	uptempo

A Funny Thing Happened on the Way to the Forum (1962)

Music and Lyrics by Stephen Sondheim

Song title, Character (Voice)	Range	Song Style
Comedy tonight, Prologus (Bar), company	A-e♭1	uptempo
Love I hear, Hero (Bar)	B-e1	ballad
Free, Pseudolus (Bar), Prologus	c-f1/c-f1 (opt. a1)	fast character
Lovely, Philia (S), Hero	c#1-f2/d-f1	ballad
Pretty little picture, Pseudolus; Hero, Philia incidental	B-f#1	uptempo
Everybody ought to have a maid, Senex (Bar), Pseudolus incidental, chorus	d-e1	uptempo
I'm calm, Hysterium (T)	d-f1	alt. fast/slow
Impossible, Senex, Hero	both B♭-g1	mod. uptempo
Bring me my bride, Miles (T), ensemble, men's chorus	B-f#	uptempo
That dirty old man, Domina (M)	b♭-f#2	uptempo
That'll show him, Philia	c1-f2	mod. uptempo
Lovely reprise, Pseudolus, Hysterium	d-f1/e-g1	ballad
Funeral sequence, Miles; Pseudolus incidental; chorus	c-e1	slow ballad
Comedy tonight reprise, company		uptempo

Gentlemen Prefer Blondes (1949)

Music by Jule Styne   Lyrics by Leo Robin

Song title, Character (Voice)	Range	Song Style
It's high time, Dorothy (M), company	b-c2	uptempo
Bye bye baby, Gus (Bar), Lorelei (M) incidental	B♭-d1	mod. uptempo
I'm just a girl from Little Rock, Lorelei	f-a1	mod. ballad
I love what I'm doing, Dorothy	a♭-c2	mod. uptempo
Just a kiss apart, Henry (T)	d-f#1	waltz ballad
It's delightful down in Chile, Beekman (Bar), Lorelei	B♭-e1/b♭-c2	mod. ballad
Sunshine, Dorothy, Henry	b♭-c2/d-f1	mod. uptempo
Park scene, chorus*		moderate
Sunshine reprise, chorus*		uptempo
I'm atingle, I'm aglow, Gage (T), ensemble incidental	d-f1	mod. uptempo

You say you care, Henry, Dorothy	db-f1/g#-bb1	ballad
Mamie is Mimi, Coles (T), Atkins (T)	both e-g1	uptempo
Coquette, solo T and A from chorus*	Ab-d1/ab-d2	cafe ballad
Diamonds are a girl's best friend, Lorelei	f-bb1	ballad
Gentlemen prefer blondes, Lorelei, Gus	a-a1/f-f1	uptempo
Homesick, ensemble		blues ballad
Keeping cool with Coolidge, Dorothy, Mrs. Spofford incidental, chorus	b-b1	Charleston
Button up with Esmond, Lorelei, chorus	g-ab1	ballad, then fast
Gentlemen prefer blondes/Diamonds are a girl's best friend reprises, company		uptempo

*Much or all in French.

George M! (1968)
Music and Lyrics by George M. Cohan

Song title, Character (Voice)	Range	Song Style
Always leave them laughing, Jerry (T), two girls incidental	g-eb1	mod. uptempo
Musical moon, Jerry, Nellie (M)	f-e1/c1-bb1	mod. uptempo
Oh, you wonderful boy, Josie (M)	c1-d2	uptempo
All aboard for Broadway, George (Bar), others incidental	d-e1	uptempo
Musical comedy man, company		mod. uptempo
All aboard for Broadway reprise, company		uptempo
Twentieth century love, company		uptempo
My home town, George	c-f1	ballad
Push me along in my pushcart, Ethel (M), two girls	unison c1-eb2	waltz ballad
A ring to the name of Rosie, four boys	TTBB	mod. ballad
Give my regards to Broadway, George, company	c#-f1	mod. uptempo
Forty-five minutes from Broadway, George, Rose (M)	A-b1/b-b1	ballad
So long Mary, ensemble	MMTBB	soft shoe ballad
Down by the Erie Canal, chorus		uptempo
Mary's a grand old name, Fay (M)	d-e1	ballad
All our friends, Sam (T), chorus	d-a1	uptempo

Montage

Yankee Doodle Dandy, George, chorus	c-f1	uptempo
Nellie Kelly, Josie, George, chorus	c1-d2/c-d1	ballad
Harrigan, George, Jerry, two boys	all c-d1	soft shoe ballad
Over there/You're a grand old flag, George, chorus	d-e1	mod. uptempo
The man who owns Broadway, George, chorus	f#-d1	ballad
I'd rather be right, George	B-d1	ballad
Finale: Give my regards/Yankee doodle, George, Agnes (M)	c-c1/c1-c2	uptempo
Bows: I want to hear a Yankee doodle tune/Give my regards, company		march, uptempo

Gigi (1973)

Music by Frederick Loewe   Lyrics by Alan Jay Lerner

Song title, Character (Voice)	Range	Song Style
Thank heaven for little girls, Honoré (Bar)	c#-d1	moving ballad
It's a bore, Gaston (Bar), Honoré	both c-d1 (much spoken)	uptempo
The earth and other minor things, Gigi (M)	b♭-d♭2	mod. uptempo
Paris is Paris again, Honoré	c-d♭1	uptempo
She is not thinking of me, Gaston	d-e1 (opt. g1)	waltz ballad
It's a bore reprise, Gaston, Honoré	both c-d1	uptempo
The night they invented champagne, Gigi, Mamita (M), Gaston	b♭-c2/f-f1/d-e1	uptempo
I remember it well, Honoré, Mamita	B♭-c1/b♭-c2	ballad
I never want to go home again, Gigi	b-c2	uptempo
Gigi, Gaston	c-e♭1	uptempo
The contract, Dufresne (Bar), Alicia (M), Mamita	all d♭-d1	uptempo, funny
I'm glad I'm not young anymore, Honoré	d♭-e♭1	mod. uptempo
In this wide, wide world, Gigi	a-d2	moving ballad
Finale: Thank heaven . . ., company		moderate

Girl Crazy (1930)

Music by George Gershwin   Lyrics by Ira Gershwin

Song title, Character (Voice)	Range	Song Style
Bidin' my time, male quartet	TTBB	easy ballad
But not for me, Kate (M)	g-b♭1	ballad
By Strauss, Zoli (Bar), women's chorus	c-f1	mod. uptempo
Could you use me, Johnny (T), men's chorus	B-a1	uptempo
Bidin' my time reprise, male quartet	TTBB	easy ballad
Bronco busters, chorus		uptempo
Embraceable you, Johnny, Molly (M), chorus	e-g1/d1-e2	ballad
I got rhythm, Kate, chorus	g-c2	uptempo
Strike up the band, Johnny, chorus	d-g2	uptempo
Sam and Delilah, Kate, chorus	g-b♭1	moderate, funny
Gay caballero, chorus		mod. uptempo
Sam and Delilah reprise, Molly, Sam (Bar)	c1-d2/spoken	mod. ballad
That lost barbershop chord, Johnny, male quartet	B♭-g1	mod. ballad
Treat me rough, Kate, Zoli	a-b♭1/c#-f#1	uptempo
But not for me reprise, Molly, Zoli	e♭1-f2/e♭-f1	ballad
Boy! What love has done for me, Kate	g-d♭2	ballad
Finale: I'm bidin' my time, company		uptempo

Godspell (1971)

Music and Lyrics by Stephen Schwartz
Additonal Music and Lyrics by Jay Hamburger and Peggy Gordon

Song title, Character (Voice)	Range	Song Style
Prologue: Tower of babble, company		moderate
Prepare ye the way of the Lord, John the Baptist (Bar)	c-d1	ballad
Save the people, Jesus (T), company	g-e1	uptempo
Day by day, Robin (M), women	c1-a1	waltz ballad
Learn your lessons well, Gilmer (Bar)	g-c1	uptempo
Bless the Lord, Joanne (S), company	g-a2	rock ballad
All for the best, Jesus, Judas (Bar)	d-g1/c-d1	uptempo
All good gifts, Lamar (T)	d-a2	ballad
Light of the world, company		uptempo
Learn your lessons well, Lamar	a-c1	uptempo
Turn back, O man, Sonia (M)	g-d2	hard ballad

Alas for you, Jesus	d-f1	uptempo
By my side, Peggy (M), Gilmar	c1-c2/c-c1	ballad
We beseech thee, Jeffrey (T), company	e-f#1 (d2 in falsetto)	uptempo
Day by day reprise, company		slow, then faster
On the willows, company		ballad
Finale, company		slow

The Golden Apple (1954)

Music by Jerome Moross   Lyrics by John Latouche

Song title, **Character (Voice)**	**Range**	**Song Style**
Nothing ever happens in Angel's Roost, Helen (M)	g#-e2	uptempo
It was a grand adventure, Ulysses (Bar)	A-f#1	moving ballad
It's the coming home together, Ulysses, Penelope (S)	d-e1/f1-g2	ballad
It's a lazy afternoon, Helen	a-d2	ballad
Oh, it's grand to see my picture in the papers, Helen, men's chorus	b-f2	uptempo
Don't give up so easy, Ulysses, chorus	d-e1	uptempo
How will we have our revenge on them, Hector (Bar)	c-d1	mod. uptempo
He brought me wildflowers, Penelope	d1-e2	mod. ballad
I've got a storebought suit, Ulysses, men's chorus	c-e1	mod. uptempo
By a goon-a, Lovely Mars (M), Ulysses, chorus	a-d2/d-d1	seductive ballad

Note: Music is continuous throught the musical; included here are excerptable portions only. The show includes a number of other solo roles, not identified here, as well as a great deal of ensemble music.

The Goodbye Girl (1993)

Music by Marvin Hamlisch   Lyrics by David Zippel

Song title, **Character (Voice)**	**Range**	**Song Style**
This is as good as it gets, Paula (M), Lucy (girl S)	both a-d♭2	mod. uptempo
No more, Paula	g♭-c2	ballad
A beat behind, Paula, Billy (T), chorus	f#-c#2/c#-f#1	mod. uptempo
My rules, Elliot (T), Paula	d♭-g♭1/a♭-c2	mod. uptempo

Good news, bad news, Elliot, Paula, Lucy	A♭-f1/a♭- e♭2/b♭-d♭2	mod. ballad
Good news, bad news reprise, Mrs. Crosby (M)	g-d2	mod. ballad
Footsteps, Paula, Lucy	e-c#2/g#-f#1	ballad
How can I win?, Paula	a♭-d♭2	ballad
Richard interred, company		uptempo
Too good to be bad, Paula, Donna (M), Jenna (M)	all a-d♭2	uptempo
2 good 2 B bad, Mrs. Crosby	b♭-e♭2	uptempo
Who would've thought?, quintet	SSSMT	jazzy uptempo
Paula, Elliot, Paula	G-e♭1/a♭-d♭2	mod. ballad
I can play this part, Elliot	g#-c#2	mod. ballad
What a guy, Paula	e-c2	ballad

Grand Hotel (1991)
Music and Lyrics by Robert Wright, George Forrest, and Maury Yeston

Song title, Character (Voice)	Range	Song Style
Grande parade, Doctor (T), Baron (T), company	c-d♭1/e♭-a♭1	mod. uptempo
At the Grand Hotel, Doctor	e♭-a♭1	mod. uptempo
Maybe my baby, Jimmy Nos. 1, 2 (T, Bar)	d-b♭1/G-f1	uptempo, jazzy
Fire and ice, Grushinskaya (M), chorus	b-c2	ballad
Twenty-two years/Villa on a hill, Raffaela (M)	f#-b	ballad
Girl in the mirror, Frieda Flaemme (M)	d-g1	slow, then fast
The crooked path, Preysing (Bar)	B-f#	character ballad
Who couldn't dance with you, Frieda, Kringelein (T)	g-g1/e-e1	uptempo
The merger is on, Zinn (Bar), chorus	e♭-d1	mod. uptempo
Love can't happen, Grushinskaya, Baron	c1-a1/d-a♭1	waltz ballad
What she needs, Doctor	f-b♭1	ballad
Bonjour amour, Grushinskaya, chorus (background)	g-b1	moving ballad
Grand Charleston, company		uptempo
We'll take a glass together, Kringelein, Baron, 2 Jimmys, chorus		uptempo
I waltz alone, Doctor, chorus	c-c1	waltz ballad
Roses at the station, Doctor	B♭-f#1	driving ballad
How can I tell her, Raffaela	b♭-b2	fast, anxious
Finale: Grand Hotel, company		mod. uptempo

Grease (1972)
Music and Lyrics by Jim Jacobs and Warren Casey

Song title, **Character (Voice)**	**Range**	**Song Style**
Rydell alma mater, chorus		anthem ballad
Rydell alma mater parody, chorus		mod. uptempo
Summer nights, Danny (T), Sandy (S), chorus	d-e♭1/d1-e♭2	uptempo
Those magic changes, Doody (T), chorus	e-f1	uptempo
Freddy my love, Marty (M), girls trio	d1-d2	easy rock ballad
Greased lightening, Kenickie (Bar), chorus	c-e♭1	fast character
Rydell's fight song, chorus		uptempo
Mooning, Roger (T), Jan (M)	f-g1/f-b♭1	blues ballad
Look at me, I'm Sandra Dee, Rizzo (M)	a-c1	ballad, character
We go together, company		uptempo
Shakin' at the high school hop, chorus		50s rock
It's raining on prom night, women's chorus		mod. ballad
Born to hand jive, Johnny Casino (Bar)	g-e1	fast uptempo
Beauty school dropout, Teen Angel (T), girls trio	e-f#1	swing ballad
Beauty school dropout reprise	e-b1 (e2 in falsetto)	swing ballad
Alone at the drive-in movie, Danny	f#-g1 (a1-d2 in falsetto)	ballad
Rock and roll party queen, Roger, Doody	both A♭-e♭1	uptempo
There are worse things I could do, Rizzo	d-b♭1	ballad
Look at me, I'm Sandra Dee reprise, Sandy	a-b2	ballad
All choked up, Danny, Sandy	F-f#1/b♭-b♭1	uptempo
We go together reprise, company		uptempo

Guys and Dolls (1950)
Music and Lyrics by Frank Loesser

Song title, **Character (Voice)**	**Range**	**Song Style**
Fugue for tinhorns, Nicely (T), Benny (T), Rusty (T)	d-a♭1/d-f1/d-f1	uptempo
Follow the fold, chorus		anthem ballad

The oldest established, men's chorus, ensemble		uptempo, funny
I'll know, Sarah (S)	eb1-f2 (opt. ab2)	ballad
A bushel and a peck, Adelaide (M), Hot Box Girls	b-d2	character, mod.
Adelaide's lament, Adelaide	ab-d2	character ballad
Guys and dolls, Nicely, Benny	both e-g1	uptempo
If I were a bell, Sarah	bb-eb2	uptempo
My time of day, Sky (Bar)	c-d1	reflective ballad
I've never been in love before, Sky, Sarah	Bb-eb1/d1-g2	ballad
Take back your mink, Adelaide, Hot Box Girls	bb-c2	mod. uptempo
Adelaide's second lament, Adelaide	d-c2	character ballad
More I cannot wish you, Arvide (Bar)	d-d1	ballad
Luck be a lady, Sky, men's chorus	db-eb1	uptempo
Sue me, Nathan (T), Adelaide	d-f1/d1-d2	ballad, funny
Sit down you're rockin' the boat, Nicely, chorus	f-bb1	fast, narrative
Marry the man today, Adelaide, Sarah	c1-c2/c1-e2	uptempo, funny
Guys and dolls reprise, company		uptempo

Gypsy (1959)

Music by Jule Styne   Lyrics by Stephen Sondheim

Song title, Character (Voice)	Range	Song Style
Some people, Rose (M)	g#-c2	uptempo
Some people reprise, Rose	g#-b1	uptempo
Small world, Rose, Herbie (Bar) incidental	f#-b1	ballad
Let me entertain you, June (girl S)	c#1-e2	mod. uptempo
Mr. Goldstone, Rose, company	f-bb1	uptempo, funny
You'll never get away from me, Rose, Herbie	f#-c2/B-c#1	mod. ballad
Farm sequence, June (S), boys	c1-f2	mod. ballad
Broadway, June, boys	e#1-d2	uptempo
If Momma was married, Louise (S), June	g-b1/g-c#2	mod. uptempo waltz
All I need is the girl, Tulsa (T)	e-g1	mod. uptempo
Everything's coming up roses, Rose	bb-c#2	uptempo
Torreadorables, girl's chorus		mod. uptempo
Together wherever we go, Rose, company	a-b1	mod. uptempo

You gotta get a gimmick, Mazeppa (M), Electra (M), Tessie (M)	g-db2/bb-db2/ bb-db2	character, hard ballad
Let me entertain you, Louise, showgirls incidental	f#-c2	slow strip ballad
Rose's turn, Rose	g-c2	driving uptempo

Hair (1968)

Music by Galt MacDermot   Lyrics by Gerome Ragni and James Rado

Song title, Character (Voice)	Range	Song Style
Aquarius, Ronny (Bar), company	eb-eb1	mod. uptempo
Donna, Berger (T), company	f-bb1	uptempo
Colored spade, Hud (Bar)	B-d1	mod. uptempo
Manchester, England, Claude (T), company	e-f#1	mod. uptempo
Ain't got no, Hud, Woof (Bar), Dionne (M)	men g#- f#1/g#1-f#2	uptempo
Dead end, quartet	all g-c2/G-c1	slow hard rock
I believe in love, Sheila (S), trio backup	g-f2	uptempo
Ain't got no grass, company		march tempo
Air, Jeanie (S); Dionne, Crissy (M) incidental	a1-g2	mod. ballad
I got life, Claude, company	d-g1	uptempo
Going down, Berger, company	c-g1	mod. ballad
Hair, Claude, company	d-g1	mod. ballad
My conviction, Margaret Mead (M)	e-a1	ballad
Easy to be hard, Sheila	c1-c2 (opt. eb2)	ballad
Don't put it down, Berger, Woof, Steve (T)	eb-eb1/g- eb1/c-ab1	country ballad
Frank Mills, Crissy	b-c#2	mod. ballad
Be-in, company		uptempo
Where do I go, Claude, company	c-f1	mod. ballad
Electric blues, quartet from chorus	SATB	mod. ballad
Black boys/White boys, chorus		uptempo
Walking in space, ensemble		rock ballad
Abie, baby, Hud, duo backup	g-b1	uptempo
The war, company		uptempo
Three-five-zero-zero, chorus		mod. uptempo
What a piece of work is man, Ronny, Walter (T)	e-a1/e-g1	ballad
Good morning Starshine, Sheila, chorus	c-bb1	moving ballad
The bed, chorus		uptempo

Song title	Range	Song Style
The flesh flowers (Let the sun shine in), chorus		mod. uptempo
Eyes look your last, Claude, Sheila, company	f#-f#1/d-f#2	mod. uptempo
Hippie life, Claude, company	c-d1	uptempo

Half a Sixpence (1963)
Music and Lyrics by David Heneker

Song title, **Character (Voice)**	**Range**	**Song Style**
Economy, male ensemble, many soli		waltz ballad
Half a sixpence, Kipps (Bar), Ann (M)	c-e♭1/d1-d2	mod. ballad
Money to burn, Kipps, men's chorus	d-g1	uptempo
I don't believe a word of it, Ann, Shopgirls	b-f2	uptempo
A proper gentleman, chorus		mod. uptempo
She's too far above me, Kipps	d-d1	ballad
If the rain's got to fall, Kipps, chorus	d♭-d♭1	mod. ballad
The old military canal, chorus		mod. uptempo
The one who's run away, Kipps, Chitterlow (Bar)	both d-e♭1	mod. uptempo
Long ago, Ann, Kipps	e1-f2/e-f1	ballad
Flash, bang, wallop!, Kipps, chorus	e♭-e1	fast character
I know what I am, Ann	d♭-b♭1	uptempo
The party's on the house, Kipps, chorus	d♭-e♭1	uptempo
Half a sixpence reprise, chorus		mod. ballad
Finale, company*		uptempo

*A pastiche of songs from the show.

Hello, Dolly (1964)
Music and Lyrics by Jerry Herman

Song title, **Character (Voice)**	**Range**	**Song Style**
Opening, chorus		mod. uptempo
I put my hand in, Dolly (S)	e♭1-g2	uptempo
It takes a woman, Horace (Bar), ensemble	B-c#1	fast, dramatic
Put on your Sunday clothes, Cornelius (T), ensemble	c-g#1	fast uptempo

Song title, Character	Range	Style
Ribbons down my back, Mrs. Molloy (M)	a-d2	ballad
Motherhood march, Dolly, Mrs. Molloy	both d1-f2	uptempo
Dancing, Dolly, Mrs. Molloy, Cornelius, Barnaby (Bar)	SATB	uptempo
Before the parade passes by, Dolly, chorus	d1-f2	uptempo
Elegance, Minnie (S), Mrs. Molloy, Cornelius, Barnaby	SATB	mod. ballad
Hello, Dolly, Dolly, men's chorus	c1-f2	mod. uptempo
It only takes a moment, Cornelius, chorus	Bb-eb1	ballad
So long, dearie, Dolly	eb1-g2	uptempo, angry
Hello, Dolly reprise, company		mod. uptempo

Hit the Deck (1927)

Music by Vincent Youmans   Lyrics by Clifford Grey and Leo Robin

Song title, Character (Voice)	Range	Song Style
The song of the Marines, men's chorus		uptempo march
Join the Navy, unison men's chorus (some soli)		mod. uptempo
Time on my hands, Bilge (T)	d-f#1	mod. ballad
Join the Navy reprise, men's chorus		mod. uptempo
The song of the Marines reprise, men's chorus		uptempo march
Loo-loo, Looloo (M)	d1-e2	mod. uptempo
Drums in my heart, Gaie (S)	bb-g2	uptempo
I know that you know, Lavinia (M)	b-e2	mod. ballad
Sometimes I'm happy, Bilge, Looloo	e-e1/e1-e2 (opt. f1, f2)	mod. uptempo
Hallelujah, company		uptempo
Through the years, Bilge	f-f1	ballad
Shore leave, chorus		uptempo waltz
The harbor of my heart, Bilge	c-g1	moving ballad
Sometimes I'm happy reprise, Looloo	f#1-f#2	mod. uptempo
Through the years reprise, Bilge	f-f1	mod. ballad
Finale, company		uptempo

How to Succeed in Business without Really Trying (1961)

Music and Lyrics by Frank Loesser

Song title, **Character (Voice)**	**Range**	**Song Style**
How to succeed . . ., Finch (T)	f-e1	uptempo
Happy to keep his dinner warm, Rosemary (M)	a-c2	moving ballad
Coffee break, chorus		uptempo
The company way, Twimble (Bar), Finch	d♭-e♭/d-g♭1	uptempo
The company way reprise, chorus		uptempo
A secretary is not a toy, Bratt (Bar), chorus	d#-e1	mod. character
Been a long day, Smitty (Bar), Rosemary, Finch	b♭-d♭1/e♭1-b♭1/g-d1	mod. ballad
Grand old Ivy, Biggley (Bar), Finch	c-d1 (opt. g1)/d-g1	uptempo march
Paris original, Rosemary, women's chorus	b♭-b♭1	ballad
Rosemary, Finch, Rosemary	e-e1/b-c2	ballad
Cinderella, darling, Smitty, women's chorus	a-b1	uptempo
Happy to keep his dinner . . . reprise, Rosemary	a-c2	moving ballad
Love from a heart of gold, Biggley, Hedy (M)	c-e♭1/c1-d2	ballad
I believe in you, Finch, men's chorus	f-g1	moving ballad
Brotherhood of man, Finch, Miss Jones (S), men	f-g1/e♭1-a♭2	uptempo
Finale: Company way, company		uptempo

I Can Get It for You Wholesale (1962)

Music and Lyrics by Harold Rome

Song title, **Character (Voice)**	**Range**	**Song Style**
I'm not a well man, Ms. Marmelstein (S), Pulvermacher (Bar)	c1-d2/c-e♭1	character
The way things are, Harry (Bar)	c-d1	fast character
When Gemini meets Capricorn, Harry, Ruthie (M)	c-e1/c1-d2	mod. uptempo
Momma, momma!, Harry, Mrs. Bogen (M)	B♭-d1/d1-d2	uptempo

The sound of money, Harry, Martha (M)	B-d1/a-d2	ballad, character
The family way, company		uptempo
Too soon, Mrs. Bogen	g-b1	ballad
Who knows, Ruthie	a♭-c2	ballad
Have I told you lately?, Meyer (Bar), Blanche (M)	B♭-e♭1/d1-e♭2	ballad
Ballad of the garment trade, company		uptempo
A gift today, company		waltz ballad
Miss Marmelstein, Ms. Marmelstein	b1-d2	fast character
On my way to love, Ruthie, Harry	c1-d2/c-d1	uptempo
What's in it for me?, Teddy (T), Martha incidental	d-d1	uptempo
What are they doing to us now, Ms. Marmelstein, chorus	a-e♭2	uptempo (in 5/4)
Eat a little something, Mrs. Bogen	g-g1	character ballad

I Do! I Do! (1966)

Music by Harvey Schmidt   Lyrics by Tom Jones

Song title, Character (Voice)	Range	Song Style
All the dearly beloved, Michael (Bar), Agnes (M)	B♭-b/a-b1	slow, recit.-like
Together forever, Michael, Agnes	G-c1/g-b♭1	waltz ballad
I do, I do, Michael, Agnes	A-e♭1/a-d2	moving ballad
Goodnight, Agnes, Michael	g-b1/G-c1	ballad
I love my wife, Michael	B♭-e♭1	jazzy ballad
Something has happened, Agnes	g-c2	ballad
My cup runneth over, Michael, Agnes	G-c1/g-c2	ballad
Love isn't everything, Michael, Agnes	G-d1/f-c2	uptempo
Nobody's perfect, Michael, Agnes	F-c1/g-d1	uptempo
It's a well known fact, Michael	a-e♭1	mod. ballad
Flaming Agnes, Agnes	g-c2	torch ballad
The honeymoon is over, Michael, Agnes	A♭-e♭1/a♭-e♭2	uptempo
Honeymoon is over/Your eyes shine like lightning, Michael, Agnes	d-d1/g-c2	mixed, mostly uptempo
Where are the snows?, Michael, Agnes	G-c1/f-c2	ballad
When the kids get married, Michael, Agnes	G-e♭1/g-e♭2	mod. uptempo
The father of the bride, Michael, Agnes	G-c1/g-g1	mostly uptempo
What is a woman?, Agnes	a-d♭2	ballad
Someone needs me, Michael, Agnes	A-a/a-c2	waltz uptempo
Roll up the ribbons, Michael, Agnes	B♭-c♭1/g#-a1	ballad
Finale: This house, Agnes, Michael	g-a1/B♭-a1	ballad

I Love My Wife (1977)

Music by Cy Coleman   Lyrics by Michael Stewart

Song title, Character (Voice)	Range	Song Style
We're still friends, chorus		uptempo
Monica, Alvin (Bar), male quartet	eb-eb1	mod. ballad
By threes, Wally (Bar), Harvey (Bar), Alan (Bar)	all d-f1	uptempo
A mover's life, Stanley (Bar), Alvin, men's chorus	c-eb1/c-f1	uptempo
Love revolution, Alvin	a#-d1	hard ballad
Someone wonderful I missed, Monica (M), Cleo (M)	bb-f1/bb-db1	ballad
Sexually free, company		uptempo, patter
Hey there, good times, men's chorus		uptempo
Lovers on Christmas eve, Monica, Wally	a-c2/a-f#1	ballad
Scream, men's chorus		march uptempo
Everybody today is turnin' on, Wally, Alvin	both d#-g#1	uptempo, patter
Married couple seeks married couple, Wally, Alvin, Cleo, Monica	c-gb1/c-bb1/ c1-gb2/c1-bb2	ballad
I love my wife, Stanley, company	Bb-g1	jazzy ballad
Bows: Hey there good times, company		uptempo

I'm Getting My Act Together
and Taking It on the Road (1978)

Music by Nancy Ford   Lyrics by Gretchen Cryer

Song title, Character (Voice)	Range	Song Style
Feel the love, Alice (M), Cheryl (M), Jake (T)	g#-c#2/g#- g#1/G#-e1	uptempo
Natural high, Heather (M), others incidental, men's chorus	a-a1	uptempo
Smile, Heather, company	c1-c#2	uptempo waltz
In a simple way I love you, Heather, others incidental	d1-b1	ballad
Miss America, Heather, company	b-d#2	mod. uptempo
Strong woman number, Alice, Heather	a-c2/db-c2	uptempo
Dear Tom, Heather	g-c2	ballad
Old friend, Heather	g-b1	ballad

Put in a package, Heather, Alice, Cheryl	b♭-c2/e1-f2/f-d2	uptempo
If only things was different, Jake	g-d1	mod. ballad
Feel the love, company		uptempo
Lonely lady, Heather	f-g1	ballad
Happy birthday, Heather, Alice, Cheryl	all b-d2	mod. uptempo
Natural high reprise, company		uptempo

Into the Woods (1987)
Music and Lyrics by Stephen Sondheim

Song title, **Character (Voice)**	**Range**	**Song Style**
Opening: Into the woods, company		mostly uptempo
Cinderella at the grave, Cinderella (S), Cinderella's Mother (M)	c1-e2/f1-f2	uptempo
Hello, little girl, Wolf (Bar), Red Riding Hood incidental	B♭-g♭1	character ballad
I guess this is goodbye, Jack (T)	d#-d#1	ballad
Maybe they're magic, Baker's Wife (M)	g#-e2	uptempo
I know things now, Red (S)	c1-e♭2	narrative ballad
A very nice prince, Cinderella, Baker's Wife	a♭-a♭1/spoken	ballad
First midnight, company		mod. uptempo
Giants in the sky, Jack	c-f#1	mod. narrative
Agony, Cinderella's Prince (Bar), Rapunzel's Prince (Bar)	both c#-e1	ballad, funny
It takes two, Baker's Wife, Baker (Bar)	a-d2/A♭-f1	ballad
Stay with me, Witch (M), Rapunzel incidental	b♭-d♭2/spoken	ballad
On the steps of the palace, Cinderella	a-d2	mod.uptempo
Finale: Into the woods, company		uptempo
Act II opening: Into the woods, company		uptempo
Agony reprise, two princes	both B-e#	ballad, funny
Any moment, Cinderella's Prince, Baker's Wife	B♭-e♭1/c1-d2	ballad
Moments in the woods, Baker's Wife	g-e♭2	uptempo
Your fault, Jack, Baker, Red, Witch, Cinderella	SSMTB	uptempo
Last midnight, Witch	b♭-d♭2	mod. uptempo
No more, Baker, Mysterious Man (Bar)	d-e♭1/G-e♭1	ballad
No one is alone, Cinderella, company	b♭-d♭2	ballad
Finale: Into the woods, company		ballad, then uptempo

Irene (1919)

Music by Harry Tierney, Charles Gaynor, Wally Harper,
Harry Carroll, Fred Fisher, Otis Clements
Lyrics by Joe McCarthy, Charles Gaynor, Harry Tierney, Jack Lloyd

Song title, **Character (Voice)**	**Range**	**Song Style**
What do you want to make those eyes at me for, chorus		mod. uptempo
The world must be bigger than an avenue, Irene (M)	b♭-c2	mod. uptempo
The family tree, Mrs. Marshall (M), women's chorus	e♭1-f2	mod. ballad
Alice blue gown, Irene	a♭-b♭1	ballad
They go wild, simply wild over me, Madame Lucy (M)	d1-d2	uptempo
An Irish girl, Irene, chorus	a-b1	ballad
Mother, angel, darling, Irene, Mrs. O'Dare (M)	f#-b♭1/g-b♭1	mod. uptempo
The last part of ev'ry party, chorus		uptempo
We're getting away with it, Lucy, Ozzie (M), Helen (M), June (M)	all c1-d2	mod. uptempo
I'm always chasing rainbows, Irene	g-a1	ballad
Irene, Donald (Bar), chorus	A-d1	mod. ballad
Greater love tango, Donald, Helen, June	c-d♭1/both c1-f2	uptempo
You made me love you, Donald, Irene	B♭-d1/b♭-c2	ballad
Alice blue gown reprise, company		mod. ballad

Jacques Brel Is Alive and Well and Living in Paris (1968)

Music by Jacques Brel　　　　　　Lyrics by Eric Blau and Mort Schuman

Song title, **Character (Voice)**	**Range**	**Song Style**
Marathon, quartet	SATB	uptempo
Alone, Man 2 (T)	G#-e♭1	mod. ballad
Madeleine, quartet	SATB	uptempo, funny
I loved, Woman 1 (S)	c1-e2	waltz ballad
Mathilde, Man 1 (Bar)	c-d1 (much spoken)	mod. uptempo
Bachelor's dance, Man 2	c-e1 (w/falsetto c2)	moving ballad
Timid Frieda, Woman 2 (M), men	a♭-d♭2	waltz ballad
My death, Woman 1	c1-c#2	ballad

Girls and dogs, men	both c#-d1	uptempo
Jackie, Man 1	d-d1	mod. ballad
Statue, Man 2	e-f1	march uptempo
The desperate ones, quartet	unison b-b1 (B-b)	ballad
Sons of ——, Woman 1	c#1-e2	waltz ballad
Amsterdam, Man 1, trio	e-f1	uptempo
The bulls, quartet	unison d-c1 (d1-c2)	mod. uptempo
Old folks, Woman 1, trio backup	eb1-db2	ballad
Marieke, Woman 1, trio hum in background	c#1-eb2	mod. ballad
Brussels, quartet	SATB	uptempo
Fanette, Man 2	c-f1	ballad
Funeral tango, Man 1	d-d1	uptempo tango
Middle class, men	c-e1/c-c#1	mod. uptempo
No love you're not alone, quartet	unison d-c1/d1-c2	mod. ballad
Next, Man 1	db-f1	recit., fast
Carousels, quartet	SATB	waltz uptempo
If we only have love, quartet	SATB	ballad

Jerry's Girls (1986)

Music and Lyrics by Jerry Herman

Song title, Character (Voice)	**Range**	**Song Style**
Just leave everything/Clothes, Dorothy (M)	e-c2	uptempo
It only takes a moment, Leslie (M)	f1-c2	mod. uptempo
Wherever he ain't, Chita (M)	f-ab1	uptempo, angry
We need a little Christmas, company		uptempo
Tap your troubles away, Dorothy, company	f#-e2	mod. uptempo
I won't send roses, Leslie	f1-d2	moving ballad
Vaudeville medley		
I was born to play the two-a-day, Dorothy	f-c2	mod. ballad
We'll always be bosom buddies, Chita, Leslie	gb-db2/gb-bb1	mod. uptempo
Man in the moon, Dorothy	a-a2	mod. ballad
So long, dearie, Chita	f#-b1	uptempo
Take it all off, company		uptempo

Song title, Character	Range	Style
Shalom/Milk and honey, Leslie, company	g-d1	ballad
Before the parade passes by, Chita	f-a♭1	uptempo, brassy
Have a nice day, Dorothy, company	a-d2	recit. ballad
Showtune, Chita, company	e-a1	uptempo
If he walked into my life, Leslie	a♭-c2	ballad
Hello, Dolly, Dorothy, company	d-a1	mod. uptempo
It's today, Leslie	g-e2	mod. uptempo
Mame, company		mod. ballad
I don't want to know, Chita	f#-b♭1 (opt. c2)	waltz ballad
Just go to the movies, company		mod. uptempo
Movies were movies/Look what happened to Mable, company (could be solo)	(f#-b♭1)	jazzy ballad
Nelson, Dorothy, company	f#-c#2	waltz ballad
Kiss her now, Leslie, Kirsten (M)	g♭-c2/g♭-a1	ballad
Mame reprise, company		mod. ballad
Time heals everything, Dorothy	d-c2	ballad
Gooch's song, Dorothy	f#-e2	character ballad
La cage aux folles, company		mod. uptempo
Song on the sand, Dorothy, company	e♭-b♭1	ballad
I am what I am, Leslie	e♭-b♭1	assertive ballad
The best of times is now, company		uptempo

Note: Premiered off-Broadway in 1981.

Jesus Christ Superstar (1971)

Music by Andrew Lloyd Webber   Lyrics by Tim Rice

Song title, Character (Voice)	Range	Song Style
Heaven on their minds, Judas (T)	d-d2	rock ballad
What's the buzz, Jesus (T), Mary Mag. (M), Apostles	f-a1/f1-a2	uptempo
Strange thing, mystifying, Judas, Jesus, Apostles	g-g1/f-c2	mod. ballad
Everything's alright, Mary, Jesus, Judas	g-b1/e-b1/B-d1	ballad
This Jesus must die, Annas (T), Caiaphas (B), High Priests	c-f1/f-f1/ TBBBB	recit.-like, ballad
Hosanna, Jesus, Caiaphas, chorus	d-f1/F-a♭	mod. uptempo
Simon Zealots, poor Jerusalem, Simon, Jesus, chorus	f-a♭1/F-a♭1	uptempo, then quiet
Pilate's dream, Pilate (Bar)	A-b♭	ballad
The temple, Jesus, chorus	B-e2	uptempo

Everything's alright reprise, Mary, Jesus	f#-a1/d-a	ballad
I don't know how to love him, Mary	a-b1	ballad
Damned for all time/Blood money, Judas, Annas, Caiphas, chorus incidental	d-d2/d-d1/G-d1	uptempo
The last supper, Jesus, Judas, Apostles	c-a1/A-c#2	ballad, then fast
Gethsemene, Jesus, Judas incidental	B♭-a♭1	hard ballad
The arrest, company		moderate
Peter's denial, Peter (T), Maid (M), Soldier (T), Old Man (B), Mary	SMTTB	moderate
Pilate and Christ, Pilate, incidental soli	B-g1	ballad
Herod's song, Herod (T)	c#-g1	fast, ragtime
Could we start again please, Mary, Peter, men	a-b1/B-f#1	ballad
Judas's death, Judas, others incidental	d-e2	uptempo
Trial by Pilate, ensemble, chorus		recit., moderate
Superstar, Judas, three "soul girls," chorus	g#-b1	uptempo

Joseph and the Amazing Technicolor Dreamcoat (1969)

Music by Andrew Lloyd Webber   Lyrics by Tim Rice

Song title, **Character (Voice)**	**Range**	**Song Style**
Jacob and sons/Joseph's coat, Narrator (M), company	b-f#2	narrative ballad
Joseph's dreams, ensemble		ballad
Poor, poor Joseph, Narrator, Brothers	c1-f2	uptempo
One more angel in heaven, Brothers		fast, Western
Potiphar, ensemble		uptempo
Close every door, Joseph (T), chorus incidental	c-f1	ballad
Go, go, go Joseph, ensemble		uptempo
Pharaoh story, Narrator, chorus	b-e2	narrative ballad
Poor, poor Pharaoh/Song of the king, Pharaoh (Bar), chorus	B-f#1	uptempo, 60s rock
Pharaoh's dreams explained, Joseph, chorus	B-e1	uptempo
Stone the crows, ensemble		uptempo
Those Caanan days, Reuben (Bar)	c-f1	moving ballad
The brothers come to Egypt/Grovel, grovel, ensemble, chorus		uptempo
Who's the thief?, Joseph, Brothers, chorus		mod. uptempo

Benjamin calypso, Brothers (many solos)		uptempo
Joseph all the time, ensemble		slow
Jacob in Egypt, ensemble		fast
Any dream will do, Joseph	c-g1	mod. ballad

The King and I (1951)

Music by Richard Rodgers   Lyrics by Oscar Hammerstein II

Song title, Character (Voice)	Range	Song Style
Whistle a happy tune, Anna (M), Louis (Bar)	b-d2/B-d1	uptempo
My lord and my master, Tuptim (S)	d#-a#2	mod. uptempo
Hello, young lovers, Anna	c#1-d2	ballad
A puzzlement, King (Bar)	d-d1	mod. ballad
Schoolroom scene, children's/women's choruses		mod. uptempo
Getting to know you, Anna, children's chorus	c#1-c#2	mod. ballad
We kiss in a shadow, Tuptim, Lun Tha (T)	d1-d2/d-d1	ballad
A puzzlement reprise, Prince (Bar), Louis	both G-a	mod. ballad
Shall I tell you what I think of you, Anna	b-c#2	uptempo, angry
Something wonderful, Lady Thiang (S)	c#1-e2	mod. ballad
Something wonderful reprise, Lady Thiang	d1-g2	mod. ballad
Western people funny, Lady Thiang, women's chorus	e1-g2	moderate, funny
I have dreamed, Lun Tha, Tuptim	c-g1/c1-g2	ballad
Hello, young lovers reprise, Anna	c1-d2	ballad
Song of the king, King, Anna incidental	d-d1	mod. ballad
Shall we dance, Anna, King incidental	d1-c2	uptempo waltz
I whistle a happy tune, children's chorus, Anna		uptempo

Kismet (1953)
Music and Lyrics by Robert Wright and George Forrest

Song title, **Character (Voice)**	**Range**	**Song Style**
Sands of time, male quintet	TTBBB	ballad
Rhymes have I, Poet (Hajj) (T), Marsinah (S)	d#-e1/e1-g2	uptempo
Fate, Poet	A-eb1	uptempo
Fate reprise, Poet	c-e1	uptempo
Bazaar of the caravans, chorus, many soli		uptempo
Not since Ninever, Lalume (S), chorus	a-bb2	uptempo
Baubles, bangles and beads, Marsinah, Caliph incidental, chorus	eb1-e2	moving ballad
Stranger in paradise, Marsinah, Caliph (T)	d1-ab2/eb-ab1	ballad
He's in love, chorus, many soli		uptempo
Gesticulate, Poet, men's chorus	B-f#1	uptempo
Finale act I: Fate reprise, company		uptempo
Night of my nights, Caliph, solo M, chorus	d-bb1/bb1-c2	waltz ballad
Stranger in paradise reprise, Marsinah	c#1-eb2	ballad
Was I Wazir?, Wazir (Bar), two guards	c-f1	character, mod.
Rahadlakum, Poet, Lalume, chorus	A-f1/d1-a2	moving ballad
And this is my beloved, Marsinah, Poet, Caliph, Wazir	STBB	ballad
The olive tree, Poet	c-eb1	uptempo
Zubbediya, Ayah (M), men's chorus	g-b1	fast character
Finale: Let peacocks and monkeys in purple adornings, company		uptempo

Kiss Me, Kate (1948)
Music and Lyrics by Cole Porter

Song title, **Character (Voice)**	**Range**	**Song Style**
Another op'nin', another show, Hattie (M), chorus	bb-f1	uptempo
Why can't you behave?, Lois (M)	f#-bb2	ballad
Wunderbar, Lilli (S), Fred (Bar)	c1-eb2/a-eb1	uptempo waltz
So in love, Lilli	c#-f#2	ballad
Padua street scene: We open in Venice, ensemble		uptempo

Song title, Character	Range	Song Style
Tom, Dick, or Harry, ensemble		uptempo
I've come to wive it, wealthily in Padua, Petruchio (T)	B♭-e♭1	character
I hate men, Katherine (S)	d1-e2	moderate, funny
Were thine that special face, Petruchio	c-f1	ballad
I sing of love, chorus, many soli		uptempo
Finale I: So kiss me, Kate, company		uptempo
Too darn hot, Paul (Bar), men's chorus	b-e1	jazzy uptempo
Where is the life that late I led?, Petruchio	B-f1	uptempo
Always true to you in my fashion, Lois	a-c2	uptempo
Bianca, chorus, many soli		mod. ballad
So in love reprise, Fred	c-f1	ballad
Brush up your Shakespeare, two gangsters (Bar)*	both c-e1	fast character
I am ashamed that women are so simple, Katherine	d1-g2	ballad
So kiss me, Kate reprise, company		uptempo
Finale: Brush up your Shakespeare, company		uptempo

*Could be performed as a solo.

Knickerbocker Holiday (1938)

Music by Kurt Weill   Lyrics by Maxwell Anderson

Song title, Character (Voice)	Range	Song Style
Washington Irving song, Irving (Bar)	c-d1 (much spoken)	narrative ballad
Clickety-clack, women's chorus		mod. uptempo
Hush, hush, Roosevelt (T), men's chorus	d-e1	narrative ballad
There's nowhere to go but up!, Brom (Bar), Tienhoven (Bar)	both B♭-e♭1	uptempo
It never was anywhere you, Brom, Tina (S)	B♭-e♭1/c1-a2	moving ballad
How can you tell an American?, Irving, Brom	both B-e1	uptempo
Will you remember me?, Tina, Brom incidental, chorus	a-g2	ballad
One touch of alchemy, Stuyvesant (Bar), chorus	d-f1	mod. uptempo
The one indispensable man, Stuyvesant, Tienhoven	B-d1/a♭-e1	fast character

Young people think about love, Tina, company	d1-d2	waltz ballad
September song, Stuyvesant	c-e♭1	ballad
All hail, the political honeymoon, company		uptempo
Ballad of the robbers, Irving	A-e1	narrative, quick
Sitting in jail, Stuyvesant	c-d1	habanera ballad
We are cut in twain, Brom, Tina	A♭-d♭1/f1-f2	quick, rhumba
There's nowhere to go . . . reprise, Irving	B♭-e♭1	mod. uptempo
To war!, men's chorus		march uptempo
Our ancient liberties, Councillors (male ensemble)		waltz ballad
May and January, chorus		ballad
The scars, Stuyvesant, chorus	G-e1	uptempo
Dirge for a soldier, chorus		anthem ballad
No, ve vouldn't gonto do it, Councillors, chorus		ballad, character
Finale: How can you tell an American?, company		uptempo

Lady in the Dark (1941)

Music by Kurt Weill   Lyrics by Ira Gershwin

Song title, **Character (Voice)**	**Range**	**Song Style**
I. Glamour dream		
Oh fabulous one, chorus		uptempo
Huxley, Sutton (Bar), Liza (M)	c#-e1/d1-d2	uptempo
One life to live, Liza	b♭-e♭2	uptempo
Girl of the moment, company		mostly uptempo
II. Wedding dream		
Mapleton High choral, chorus		anthem ballad
This is new, Randy (Bar)	B♭-e♭1	ballad
The princess of pure delight, Liza, company	c1-e2	narrative ballad
III. Circus dream		
The greatest show on earth, Ringmaster (T), chorus	d-e1	uptempo
The best years of his life, Ringmaster, Randy, Liza, chorus	c-e1/B♭-d1/b♭-e♭2	waltz ballad
Tschaikowsky, Ringmaster, chorus incidental	d-g1	uptempo

The saga of Jenny, Liza, unison chorus	c1-e♭2	moving ballad
IV. Childhood dream		
My ship, Liza	c1-f2	ballad

Li'l Abner (1956)

Music by Gene de Paul   Lyrics by Johnny Mercer

Song title, **Character (Voice)**	**Range**	**Song Style**
A typical day, chorus		mod. uptempo
If I had my druthers, Abner (T), men's chorus	e-c1	bouncy ballad
If I had my druthers reprise, Daisy (M)	e1-c2	bouncy ballad
Jubilation T. Cornpone, Marryin' Sam (T), chorus	d-g1	uptempo
Rag off'n the bush, chorus		uptempo
Namely you, Daisy, Li'l Abner	c1-e♭2/e♭-g1	ballad
Unnecessary town, company		uptempo
What's good for General Bullmoose, Secretaries (women's chorus)		mod. uptempo
The country's in the very best of hands, Li'l Abner, Marryin' Sam, chorus	e-e1/d-g1	uptempo
Oh happy day, Scientists (men's trio)	all d-e1	uptempo
Past my prime, Daisy, Marryin' Sam	d1-c2/d-e♭1	moving ballad
Love in a home, Li'l Abner, Daisy	c-f1/b♭-f2	ballad
Progress is the root of all evil, Gen. Bullmoose (Bar)	e-d1	mod. uptempo
Progress . . . reprise, Gen. Bullmoose	d#-d1	mod. uptempo
Put 'em back, Wives (women's chorus)		fast character
Stomp, Marryin' Sam, chorus	f-f1	uptempo
Cornpone, company		uptempo

Little Johnny Jones (1904)

Music and Lyrics by George M. Cohan

Song title, **Character (Voice)**	**Range**	**Song Style**
The Cecil in London Town, company		mod. uptempo
Then I'd be satisfied with life, Anstey (Bar)	c-e♭1	mod. narrative ballad
Yankee doodle boy, Johnny (T), chorus	e-g1	uptempo
Oh, you wonderful boy, Goldie (M), Flo (M), girls	d1-e2/e1-c2	mod. uptempo

The voice in my heart, Mrs. Kenworth (S), girls	d-c♭3	waltz ballad
Yankee doodle reprise, Wilson (Bar), McGee (T)	both f-d1	uptempo
Finale act I: Good luck, Johnny, company		uptempo
Captain of a ten day boat, Captain (Bar), chorus	B♭-d1	fast character
Goodbye Flo, Flo, men's chorus	a-d♭2	mod. ballad
Funny proposition, Johnny	d#-e1	mod. uptempo
Let's you and I just say goodbye, Goldie	d1-g2	ballad
Give my regards to Broadway, Johnny, chorus	d-f1	mod. uptempo
American ragtime, McGee, Flo, chorus	d-g1/f1-e2	mod. ragtime
Voice in my heart reprise, Captain, Mrs. Kenworth	c-d1/d1-b♭2	ballad
Finale act II, company		mod. uptempo

Note: Substantially revised in 1980.

Little Mary Sunshine (1959)
Music and Lyrics by Rick Besoyan

Song title, **Character (Voice)**	**Range**	**Song Style**
The forest ranger, Capt. Jim (Bar), men's chorus	g-d1	uptempo march
Little Mary Sunshine, Mary (S), solo S, chorus	d1-d2/d1-c2	mod. ballad
Look for a sky of blue, Mary, men's chorus	c1-e♭2	mod. ballad
You're the fairest flower, Capt. Jim	G-d1	mod. ballad
In Izzen Schnooken, Madame Ernestine (M)	b♭-c2	character ballad
Playing croquet, unison women's chorus		mod. waltz ballad
Swinging, chorus, many soli		mod. waltz
Tell a handsome stranger, chorus		mod. uptempo
Once in a blue moon, Billy (Bar), Nancy (M)	B♭-e♭1/spoken	mod. uptempo
Colorado love call, Capt. Jim, Mary	A-f1/a-e2	mod. ballad
Every little nothing, Mme. Ernestine, Mary	g-a1/b-d2	mod. uptempo
What has happened, company		uptempo
Such a merry party, chorus		uptempo

Say uncle, Oscar (Bar), women's chorus	c#-d1	mod. character
Heap big Injun, Chief (Bar)	B♭-d♭1	fast character
Naughty, naughty Nancy, Mary, women's chorus	c1-f2	mod. uptempo
Mata Hari, Nancy, Oscar	b-c2/B-d1	waltz ballad
Do you ever dream of Vienna?, Mme. Ernestine, chorus	b-c2	mod. ballad
Coo-coo, Mary, chorus	d1-a1	character ballad
Colorado love call reprise, Capt. Jim, company	B♭-f1	mod. ballad
Forest rangers reprise, men's chorus		uptempo march
Finale:When e'er a cloud appears, company		uptempo

Little Me (1962)

Music and Lyrics by Carolyn Leigh and Cy Coleman

Song title, Character (Voice)	Range	Song Style
The truth, Patrick (Bar), Belle (M), men's chorus	A-d1/a-c2	uptempo
I love you, Noble (T), Young Belle (M), chorus	d♭-f1/d♭1-e2	mod. ballad
Their side of the tracks, Young Belle	a-d2	uptempo
Deep down inside, Young Belle, Pinchley (T), Junior (T), chorus	b♭-f#2/B♭-f#1/ d-f#1	mostly uptempo
To be a performer, Bernie (T), Bennie (T), Belle	d-g1/d-g1/d-f	uptempo
Oh! Dem dimples!, Belle, men's chorus	b♭-d2	soft shoe ballad
Boom boom, Val (S), women's chorus	c#1-g2	fast character
I've got your number, George (Bar)	e♭-f♭1	mod. uptempo
Real live girl, Fred (Bar), chorus	d-c1	waltz ballad
I love sinking you, Noble, Young Belle	c-f1/c1-f2	ballad
Poor little Hollywood star, Young Belle	g-e2	mod. ballad
Be a performer reprise, Bennie, Bernie	both e-e1	mod. uptempo
Little me, Belle, Young Belle	a-c#2/a-c#2	mod. ballad
Goodbye, Prince (T), chorus	B-f#1	character ballad
Here's to us, Belle, men's chorus	f-b♭1	mod. uptempo

A Little Night Music (1973)
Music and Lyrics by Stephen Sondheim

Song title, Character (Voice)	Range	Song Style
Overture, Liebeslieders	SSMTB	mod. uptempo
Night waltz, Liebeslieders	SSMTB	mod. ballad
Now, Frederick (Bar), Anne (S)	B♭-e1/spoken	uptempo, patter
Later, Henrick (T)	b#-b1	uptempo
Soon, Anne, Henrik, Frederick	c#1-g#2/g-a1/ b-d	mod. ballad
The glamorous life, Frederika (girl S), Desiree (S), Madame Arnfeldt (M), Liebeslieders	d1-e♭2/e1-a2/c- e♭1	uptempo
Remember, Liebeslieders	SSMTB	waltz ballad
You must meet my wife, Frederick, Desiree	c-e♭1/c1-e2	mod. waltz
Liaisons, Mme. Arnfeldt	d-f1*	slow, inward
In praise of women, Carl Magnus (Bar)	c#-f1	uptempo
Every day a little death, Charlotte (M), Anne	both g#-b1	ballad
A weekend in the country, company		uptempo
Night waltz reprise, Liebeslieders	SSMTB	mod. ballad
It would have been wonderful, Frederick, Carl Magnus	both c-e1	ballad, funny
Perpetual anticipation, Liebeslieder women	SSM	uptempo, charming
Send in the clowns, Desiree	g♭-a♭1	ballad
The miller's son, Petra (M)	f#-b1	ballad, with faster parts

* Notated an octave higher.

Little Shop of Horrors (1982)
Music by Alan Menken   Lyrics by Howard Ashman

Song title, Character (Voice)	Range	Song Style
Little shop of horrors, Chiffon (S), Crystal (M), Ronnette (M)	e1-d2/e1-d2/b- g1	mod. ballad
Skid row (Downtown), company		mod. uptempo
Grow for me, Seymour (T)	B♭-f1	50s rock ballad
Don't it go to show ya never know, ensemble		jazzy uptempo
Somewhere that's green, Audrey (M)	b-c2	ballad

Closed for renovations, Seymour,	Bb-g1/bb-c2/	uptempo
Audrey, Mushnik (Bar)	Bb-f1	
Dentist!, Orin (Bar), women's trio	G-e1	uptempo
Mushnik and son, Mushnik, Seymour	G-eb1/e-g1	mod. uptempo
Feed me (Git it), Seymour, Audrey II	g-g1/bb-g2	driving uptempo
(S)		
Now (It's just the gas), Seymour, Orin	Bb-gb1/f#-eb1	uptempo, patter
Call back in the morning, Seymour,	B#-d#1/b-c#2	mod. uptempo
Audrey		
Suddenly, Seymour, Seymour, Audrey	A-c#1/a-c#2	mod. ballad
Suppertime, Audrey II, women's trio	g-f1	uptempo
The meek shall inherit, company		mod. uptempo
Finale: Don't feed the plants, company		uptempo

Lost in the Stars (1949)

Music by Kurt Weill   Lyrics by Maxwell Anderson

Song title, **Character (Voice)**	**Range**	**Song Style**
The hills of Ixopo, Leader (T), chorus	d-e1	narrative ballad
Thousands of miles, Stephen (Bar)	A-c1	ballad
Train to Johannesburg, Leader, chorus	d-g1	uptempo
The search, men's chorus, many soli		mod. uptempo
The little gray house, Stephen, chorus	Ab-db1	narrative ballad
Who'll buy?, Linda (M), chorus	bb-db2	character
Trouble man, Irina (S)	c1-f2	ballad
Murder in Parkwold, double chorus		uptempo
Fear!, chorus, many soli		driving uptempo
Lost in the stars, Stephen, chorus	Ab-c1 (opt. f1)	ballad
The wild justice, Leader, chorus	d-ab1	mod. ballad
O Tixo, Tixo help me!, Stephen	d-f1	soliloquy
Stay well, Irina	c1-f2	ballad
Cry the beloved country, Leader, M	a-e1/a1-e2	moving ballad
solo, chorus		
Big mole, Alex (Bar)	Bb-c1	character
A bird of passage, Bar solo, chorus	eb-eb1	mod. ballad
Finale: Each lives in a world of dark,		mod. uptempo
company		

Mack and Mabel (1974)
Music and Lyrics by Jerry Herman

Song title, **Character (Voice)**	**Range**	**Song Style**
Movies were movies, Mack (Bar)	A-d1	mod. uptempo
Look what happened to Mabel, company		uptempo
Big time, Lottie (M), chorus	e-b1	uptempo
I won't send roses, Mack, Mabel (M)	G-c1/g-d1	ballad
I want to make the world laugh, Mack, chorus	A-e1	ballad
Wherever he ain't, Mabel	a-d2	mod. uptempo
Hundreds of girls, Mack, women's chorus	A-f#1	uptempo
When Mabel comes in the room, company		mod. uptempo
Hit 'em on the head, Mack, Kleinman (T), Fox (T), men's chorus	all B-f1	mod. uptempo
Time heals everything, Mabel	f#-d2	ballad
Tap your troubles away, Lottie, women's chorus	f-b♭1	mod. uptempo shuffle
Happy ending, Mack	G-d1	mod. ballad

Mame (1966)
Music and Lyrics by Jerry Herman

Song title, **Character (Voice)**	**Range**	**Song Style**
St. Bridget, Agnes (M), Patrick (boy S) incidental	b-f2	slow, quasi-character
It's today, Mame (M), chorus	a-f2	uptempo
Open a new window, Mame, Patrick, chorus	f1-c2/c1-c2	mod. uptempo
The moon song, Vera (M), women's chorus	g-a1	character ballad
My best girl, Patrick, Mame	a♭-c2/g-c2	ballad
We need a little Christmas, Mame; Agnes, Ito, Patrick at end	f-b♭1	uptempo
The fox hunt, chorus		uptempo
Mame, Beau (Bar), chorus	d-c#1	mod. ballad
Opening act II: Letters, Patrick (boy), Patrick (T)	d-b♭1/g-d1	slow, epistolary ballad
My best girl reprise, Patrick	c-e1	mod. ballad

Bosom buddies, Mame, Vera	both e♭-b♭1	moderate, funny
Gooch's song, Agnes	g-c2	ballad, funny
That's how young I feel, Mame, ensemble	g-b♭1	uptempo
If he walked into my life, Mame	f#-b♭1	ballad
It's today reprise, Mame, chorus	a-b♭1	uptempo
Finale: Open a new window/Today, company		uptempo

Man of La Mancha (1965)

Music by Mitch Leigh   Lyrics by Joe Darion

Song title, Character (Voice)	Range	Song Style
Man of la Mancha (I, Don Quixote), Don Quixote (Bar), Sancho (T)	c-e1/d-g1	uptempo, driving
It's all the same, Aldonza (M), Muleteers incidental	e♭-a♭2	angry uptempo
Dulcinea, Don Q., Muleteers	B-e1	ballad
I'm only thinking of him, Antonia (M), Padre (T), Housekeeper (M)	c1-f2/g-g1/f-e♭2	moving ballad
We're only thinking of him, as before w/ Dr. Carracco (Bar)	MMTB	moving ballad
I really like him, Sancho	g-g1	character ballad
What does he want of me?, Aldonza	d1-f2	moving ballad
Little bird, little bird, Muleteers (male ensemble)		ballad
Barber's song, Barber (T)	f-g1	character
Golden helmet of Mambrino, Don Q., Barber; Sancho incidental, chorus	B-d1/d-e1	uptempo
To each his Dulcinea, Padre	c-f1	ballad
The impossible dream, Don Q.	c-e♭1	ballad
Knight of the woeful countenance, Innkeeper (Bar), chorus	B-c#1	uptempo
Man of la Mancha reprise, Don Q.	c-d1	uptempo
Aldonza, Aldonza	a♭1-e2	angry uptempo
A little gossip, Sancho	c-f1	mod. funny
Dulcinea reprise, Aldonza	g1-f2	ballad
Man of la Mancha reprise, Don Q., Sancho, Aldonza	men: c-c1/her: c1-c2	uptempo
The psalm, Padre	f-f1	anthem ballad
Finale: The impossible dream, company		ballad

March of the Falsettos (1981)

Music and Lyrics by William Finn

Song title, Character (Voice)	Range	Song Style
Four Jews in a room bitching, Marvin (Bar), Mendel (Bar), Jason (boy S), Whizzer (T)		uptempo
Tight-knit family, Marvin	c#-e1	moving ballad
Love is kind, Mendel, company	G#-e1	moving ballad
Thrill of first love, Whizzer, Marvin	G#-f#1/g#-d#1	mod. uptempo
Marvin at the pyschiatrist's, Jason, Marvin, Mendel	a-c2/B-f1/d-f1	recit. ballad
My father's a homo, Jason, Trina (M), Marvin; Whizzer incidental	a-b1/b-d2/d-d1	mod. uptempo
I'm breaking down, Trina	g#-c2	moving ballad
Please come to our house, Jason, Trina, Mendel	b-c#2/b-e2/B-c#1	uptempo
Breakfast over sugar, Marvin, Trina	G-c1/g-c2	ballad
Jason's therapy (Feel alright), company		mod. ballad
Marriage proposal, Mendel	c-e2	mod. ballad
Tight-knit family reprise, Marvin, Mendel	c#-d1/c#-e1	mod. ballad
Trina's song, Trina	a-d#2	ballad
The chess game, Marvin, Whizzer	A-d#1/A-f1	waltz ballad
Making a home, Trina, Mendel, Whizzer incidental	c1-eb2/e-eb1	moving ballad
The games I play, Whizzer	B-g1	driving ballad
Marvin hits Trina, company		uptempo
I never wanted to love you, company		mod. uptempo
Father to son, Jason, Marvin; Mendel incidental	g-bb1/A-c1	ballad

Note: See also *Falsettoland*, the second half of the musical *Falsettos* (1992) of which this show is the first half.

Maytime (1917)

Music by Sigmund Romberg   Lyrics by Rida Johnson Young and Cyrus Wood

Song title, Character (Voice)	Range	Song Style
Tap, fellows, tap, men's chorus		uptempo

In our little home, sweet home, Ottillie (S), Richard (T)	d1-b2/d-g1	uptempo
It's a windy day on the battery, Matthew (T), women's chorus incidental	d-g1	uptempo waltz
Gypsy song, Rudolpho (T)	d-a1	waltz ballad
Sweetheart, will you remember?, Ottillie, Richard	e♭1-b♭2/e-a♭1	ballad
Jump, Jim Crow, Matthew	e-f#1	mod. uptempo
The road to paradise, Ottillie, Richard	e♭1-a♭2/e♭-g♭1	ballad
Old things, old things, unison chorus		uptempo
Will you remember reprise, Ottillie	c1-g2 (opt. b♭2)	ballad
Since the war in Europe, unison women's chorus*		uptempo
Dancing will keep you young, Ermintrude (M), Matthew	e♭1-g2/f-g1	uptempo waltz
Go away, girls, Richard	e-f1	mod. ballad
Sweetheart, will you remember reprise, Richard	b♭-g2 (opt. b♭2)	ballad

*In several languages: Spanish, French, and English.

Me and Juliet (1953)

Music by Richard Rodgers   Lyrics by Oscar Hammerstein II

Song title, Character (Voice)	Range	Song Style
A very special day, Jeanie (M)	c1-e2	ballad
That's the way it happens, Jeanie, Larry (T)	b-c#2/e♭-f1	uptempo
Marriage type love, Charlie (Bar); Juliet (S), chorus incidental	d-e1	ballad
Marriage type love reprise, Juliet, Charlie	e♭1-g2/e♭-e♭1	ballad
Keep it gay, Bob (T), women's chorus; then chorus	d-e1	fast, calypso
Keep it gay reprise, Betty (M)	b♭-c1	uptempo
The big black giant, Larry	d♭-e♭1	uptempo
No other love, Jeanie, Larry	d1-a♭2/d-a♭1	tango ballad
The big black giant reprise, Ruby (M)	c1-c2	uptempo
It's me, Betty, Jeanie	both c1-d♭2	uptempo, funny
No other love reprise, Juliet	e♭1-a♭2	tango ballad
Intermission, chorus, many soli		uptempo
It feels good, Bob	c-f1	uptempo

We deserve each other, Carmen (M)	b♭-c2	uptempo
I'm your girl, Jeanie, Larry	d♭1-f2/e♭-f1	ballad
Marriage type love reprise, Betty, chorus	e♭1-f2	ballad

Me and My Girl (1986)

Music by Noel Gay Lyrics by L. Arthur Rose and Douglas Furber

Song title, **Character (Voice)**	**Range**	**Song Style**
A weekend in Hareford, company		uptempo
Thinking of no one but me, Jacquie (S), Gerald (T)	b♭-c2/f-f#1	mod. ballad
The family solicitor, Parchester (T), ensemble	d-g1	fast character
Me and my girl, Bill (Bar), Sally (M)	B♭-c1/f-d2	mod. uptempo
An English gentleman, Staff (ensemble)		mod., funny
You would if you could, Jacquie, Bill	c-e2/spoken	mod. ballad
Hold my hand, Bill, Sally	c-d1/c1-c2	moving ballad
Once you lose your heart, Sally	a♭-d♭1	ballad
The fugue, company		uptempo
The Lambeth walk, Bill, company	c-e1	swing uptempo
The sun has got his hat on, Gerald, company	e-g1	uptempo
Take it on the chin, Sally	a-c2	mod. uptempo
Once you lose your heart reprise, Sally	a♭-d♭1	ballad
Song of Hareford, Duchess (M), Ancestors (TTBB)	a-f2	narrative ballad
Love makes the world go round, Bill, Sir John (Bar), Ancestors	both c#-f1	uptempo
Leaning on a lamppost, Bill	B♭-e1	swing ballad
The world keeps on turning, company		uptempo
Bows: Me and my girl/Lambeth walk, company		mod. uptempo

Merrily We Roll Along (1981)
Music and Lyrics by Stephen Sondheim

Song title, Character (Voice)	Range	Song Style
The hills of tomorrow, chorus		anthem ballad
Merrily we roll along, company		uptempo
Rich and happy, Frank (T), Mary (M), company	c-e1/c1-c2	moderate
Old friends/Like it was, Mary	f-c2	jazzy ballad
Franklin Shepard, Inc., Charley (T)	d♭-g♭1	fast character
Old friends, Frank, Charley, Mary	men: B♭-e♭1/a♭-f#2	jazzy ballad
Not a day goes by, Beth (S)	d1-f#2	ballad
Now you know, Mary, company	a♭-d2	uptempo
It's a hit, Frank, Mary, Charley, Joe (T)	SATB (all need g1/g2)	uptempo
The blob, Gussie (Bar)	B-d1	uptempo
Good thing going, Charley	B-d1	ballad
The blob reprise, company*		alt. slow/fast
Bobby and Jackie and Jack, Frank, Mary, Charley, Piano Player incidental	STBB	uptempo
Not a day goes by reprise, Frank, Mary	e-e1/f#-e2	ballad
Opening doors, company		uptempo
Our time I, Frank	d♭-g♭1	ballad
Our time II, Frank, Charley	d♭-g♭1/B♭-g♭1	ballad
Our time III, company		ballad
The hills of tomorrow reprise, company		uptempo

*Combines "The Blob" with "Good Thing Going."

The Merry Widow (1907)
Music by Franz Lehar   Lyrics by Adrian Ross

Song title, Character (Voice)	Range	Song Style
Now, ladies and gentlemen, chorus		uptempo
A dutiful wife, Natalie (S), Camille (T)	d1-g2/d-b♭1	uptempo
In Marsovia, Sonia (S), chorus	b-b2	uptempo
Maxim's, Danilo (T)	A-g1	uptempo
Home, Camille	e-a1	mod. uptempo
Ladies, choice!, company		uptempo waltz
I bid you wait, chorus		mod. uptempo

Vilia, Sonia	d1-b2	mod. uptempo
The cavalier, Sonia, Danilo incidental	e1-a2	uptempo
Women, male sextet	TTTBBB	march uptempo
Love in my heart, Camille	f-a1 (opt. c2)	ballad
Ha! Ha! Ha!, company		uptempo
The girls at Maxim's, Zozo (M), female sextet, chorus	b-e2	saucy uptempo
Quite Parisian, Nisch (Bar), chorus	c-e1	character ballad
I love you so, Sonia, Danilo	d1-a2/d-f#1	ballad
You may study her ways, company		march uptempo

Milk and Honey (1961)

Music and Lyrics by Jerry Herman

Song title, **Character (Voice)**	**Range**	**Song Style**
Sheep song, chorus, many soli		mod. uptempo
Shalom, Phil (T), Ruth (S)	A-e1/bb-ab2	mod. uptempo
Hora I, chorus		uptempo
Hora II, Phil, chorus	e-f#1	uptempo
Milk and honey, David (T), chorus	A-g#1	mod. ballad
There's no reason in the world, Phil	c#-f#1	ballad
Chin up, ladies, Mrs. Perlman (M), Mrs. Weiss (M), Mrs. Segal (M)	all e-c2	mod. character
That was yesterday, Ruth, company	bb-d2	ballad
Let's not waste a moment, Phil	A-f1	uptempo
The wedding, company		uptempo
Like a young man, Phil, men's chorus	A-f#1	ballad
I will follow you, David	d-bb1	mod. ballad
Hymn to Hymie, Mrs. Weiss	ab-c2	mod. character
There's no reason . . . reprise, Ruth	a-g2	ballad
Milk and honey reprise, Adi (S), chorus	e1-g2	mod. ballad
As simple as that, Phil, Ruth	c-d1/c1-e2	ballad
There's a short forever, Phil; Ruth incidental	A-f1	uptempo

M'lle Modiste (1905)

Music by Victor Herbert   Lyrics by Henry Blossom

Song title, **Character (Voice)**	**Range**	**Song Style**
Furs and feathers, Nanette (M), Fanchette (S), women's chorus	d1-f#2/f#1-b2	sprightly uptempo

When the cat's away the mice will play, Fanchette, Nanette, Madame. Cecile (A)	d1-a2/c1-g2/f-c2	ballad
The time and the place and the girl, Etienne (T), chorus	e1-a2	march uptempo
If I were on the stage (Kiss me again), Fifi (S)	b-c3	uptempo
Love me, love my dog, Gaston (T)	e-g1	character ballad
Hats make the woman, Fifi, women's chorus	c#1-g2	character ballad
No she shall not go alone, company		uptempo
Footmen's chorus, men's chorus		march uptempo
I want what I want when I want it, Count (Bar), chorus	B-e1	moving ballad
Gladly we respond, chorus	e♭-f1	march uptempo
Ze English language, Gaston	d1-a2	character ballad
The mascot of the troop, Fifi, men's chorus	G-c1	march uptempo
The dear little girl who is good, René (Bar)	b-e2	ballad
The Keokuk culture club, Mrs. Bent (M), chorus	c#1-a2 (opt. b2) d1-b2	character
The nightingale and the star, Fifi		uptempo waltz
Hark the drum, Fifi, chorus		uptempo

The Most Happy Fella (1956)
Music and Lyrics by Frank Loesser

Song title, Character (Voice)	Range	Song Style
Ooh! My feet, Cleo (M)	b♭-b♭1	character
Somebody, somewhere, Rosabella (S)	e1-g2	moving ballad
The most happy fella, Postman (Bar), Tony (Bar), chorus	e-e1/e-g1	uptempo
Standing on the corner, Barbershop quartet		ballad
Joey, Joey, Joey, Joe (Bar)	d♭-f1	mod. ballad
Rosabella, Tony	d-f1	waltz ballad
Abbondanza, TTB trio*		fast character
Sposalizio, chorus		uptempo
Benvenuta, TTB trio		uptempo
Don't cry, Joe	c-e♭1	ballad
Fresno beauties, company		uptempo
Love and kindness, Doc (T)	e♭-a♭1	waltz ballad

Happy to make your acquaintance, Rosa, Tony	d1-e2/c#-e1	ballad
I don't like this dame, Marie (M), Cleo	e♭1-d2/b♭-c2	uptempo
Big D, Cleo, Herman (Bar)	c1-a2/d-a♭1	fast character
How beautiful the days, Rosa, Marie, Tony, Joe	SMBB	ballad
Young people, Marie	c1-e2	uptempo
Warm all over, Rosa	c#1-f#2	ballad
I like everybody, Herman, Cleo incidental	g-g1	uptempo
My heart is so full of you, Tony, Rosa	d♭-f1/f1-g♭2	moving ballad
Mamma, mamma, Tony	c#-g1	ballad
Abbondanza reprise, TTB trio		uptempo
Goodbye, darlin', Cleo, Herman	g#-b1/f-f1	mod. uptempo
Song of a summer night, Doc, chorus	f#-f#1	ballad
Please let me tell you, Rosa	e1-e2	ballad
Nobody's ever gonna love you, Marie, Tony, Cleo		uptempo
I made a fist!, Cleo, Herman	d1-b♭1/f-a♭1	character
My heart is so full of you, company		mod. uptempo

*In Italian.

Music in the Air (1932)

Music by Jerome Kern   Lyrics by Oscar Hammerstein II

Song title, **Character (Voice)**	**Range**	**Song Style**
Melodies of May, chorus*		slow
I've told every little star, Karl (Bar)	c-e♭1	mod. ballad
Prayer, Sieglinde (M), chorus	b-e1	ballad
There's a hill beyond a hill, chorus		madrigal-like
At Stony Brook, Cornelius (T), chorus	B♭-f1	mod. ballad
I am so eager, Frieda (S)	d1-b♭2	uptempo waltz
I've told every little star, Sieglinde, Karl	c1-f2/c-e♭1	ballad
Tingle-tangle, Bruno (T), Frieda, chorus incidental	d-f1/b♭-g2	uptempo
In Egern on the Tegern see, Marthe (M)	g-f2	ballad
One more dance, Bruno	c#-f#1	waltz ballad
Episode of the swing, company		uptempo
Night flies by, Frieda, Bruno	c#1-a2/c-f#1	ballad
I'm alone, Frieda	b♭-d2	ballad
When spring is in the air, Sieglinde, chorus	d1-g2	uptempo

In Egern on the Tegern see reprise, Lilli (M)	a-e♭2	ballad
The song is you, Bruno	c-f1	moving ballad
The song is you reprise, Frieda, Bruno	d1-g2/e-g1	ballad
The village of Edendorf, company		uptempo

*Beethoven's Op. 2, No. 3, arranged by Kern.

The Music Man (1961)
Music and Lyrics by Meredith Willson

Song title, Character (Voice)	Range	Song Style
Rock Island, male ensemble	spoken	uptempo, patter
Iowa stubborn, chorus, many soli		mod. uptempo
Ya got trouble, Harold (Bar), chorus	A♭-e♭1	uptempo
Piano lesson/If you don't mind my saying so, Marian (S), Mrs. Paroo (M)	a♭-d2/d1-e♭2	ballad, character
Goodnight my someone, Marian	b-e2	ballad
Seventy-six trombones, Harold, chorus	B-f1	uptempo march
Sincere, Barbershop quartet	TTBB	ballad
The sadder but wiser girl, Harold, Marcellus (T) incidental	d-e1 (much spoken)	character
Pick-a-little, talk-a-little, Townsladies, Barbershop quartet		uptempo
Marian the librarian, Harold	B♭-f1	moving ballad
My white knight, Marian	c1-f#2	ballad
The Wells Fargo wagon, chorus, many soli		uptempo
It's you, Barbershop quartet	TTBB	ballad
Shipoopi, Marcellus	g-a1	uptempo
Pick-a-little reprise, Townsladies		uptempo
Lida Rose/Will I ever tell you, Marian, barbershop quartet	d1-f#2	ballad
Gary, Indiana, Winthrop (boy S); Marian, Mrs. Paroo incidental	c1-e♭2	character ballad
Lida Rose reprise, Barbershop quartet	TTBB	ballad
Till there was you, Marian, Harold	d1-g2/e♭-c1	ballad
Goodnight my someone/76 trombones, company		uptempo

My Fair Lady (1956)

Music by Frederick Loewe   Lyrics by Alan Jay Lerner

Song title, Character (Voice)	Range	Song Style
Why can't the English?, Higgins (Bar)	B-d1	uptempo
Wouldn't it be loverly?, Eliza (S), chorus	c1-e♭2	ballad
With a little bit of luck, Doolittle (Bar), Jamie (T), Harry (Bar)	G-d1/c-e1/e-g	fast character
I'm an ordinary man, Higgins	B♭-b♭	uptempo
With a little bit . . . reprise, Doolittle, chorus	G-e1	fast character
Just you wait, Eliza	c1-e♭2	uptempo, angry
The servant's chorus, ensemble	SATTBB	mod. uptempo
The rain in Spain, Eliza, Higgins, Pickering (Bar)	c1-f2/men: c-f1	uptempo
I could have danced all night, Eliza	b-g2	uptempo
Ascot gavotte, chorus		stately ballad
On the street where you live, Freddy (T)	c-e1	ballad
You did it, Pickering, Higgins, servants	c-e1/c-f1	uptempo
On the street . . . reprise, Freddy	c-e1	ballad
Show me, Eliza	d1-g2	uptempo
The flower market, chorus		ballad
Get me to the church on time, Doolittle, chorus	B-d1	uptempo
A hymn to him, Higgins	B-d1	uptempo
Without you, Eliza	b-e♭2	uptempo
I've grown accustomed to her face, Higgins	A-b♭1	ballad/ends fast

My Favorite Year (1993)

Music by Stephen Flaherty   Lyrics by Lynn Ahrens

Song title, Character (Voice)	Range	Song Style
20 million people, company		mod. uptempo
Larger than life, Benjy (T)	e♭-e♭1	uptempo
Musketeer sketch, company		mod. uptempo
Rookie in the ring, Belle (M)	g-b♭1	mod. uptempo
Manhattan, Swann (Bar), chorus	G-d1	uptempo
The gospel according to King, King (Bar)	B-c#1	uptempo
Funny/The joke, KC (M), Alice (M)	a-e#2/f#-b1	uptempo, funny
Welcome to Brooklyn, company		uptempo

If the world were like the movies, Swann	G#-d1	mod. ballad
Exits, Swann	G-d♭1	ballad
Shut up and dance, KC, Benjy, chorus incidental	a-c2/g-d1	mod. uptempo
Professional showbizness comedy, King, Alice, chorus (clowns)	c-d1/b-b1	mod. uptempo
Comedy cavalcade theme, chorus		mod. uptempo
My favorite year, Benjy, company	d♭-g♭1	mod. uptempo

My One and Only (1983)

Music by George Gershwin   Lyrics by Ira Gershwin and B. G. DeSylva

Song title, Character (Voice)	Range	Song Style
I can't be bothered now, company		uptempo
Boy wanted/Soon, Edythe (M), Billy (Bar)	g-d2/c-e1	moving ballad
High hat, Billy, Mr. Magix (Bar), men's chorus	d-d1/c-e♭1	mod. ballad
He loves and she loves, Billy, Edythe, men's chorus on reprise	A-b/a-c2	moving ballad
Flying, male ensemble ("New Rhythm Boys")		uptempo
'S wonderful, Billy, Edythe	c-c#1/c1-c2	mod. ballad
Finale: Strike up the band, Billy	c-d1	ballad, then fast
In the swim/What are we here for, female sextet	SSSAAA	uptempo
Nice work if you can get it, Edythe	g#-b1	mod. ballad
My one and only, Billy, Mr. Magix	both d-e♭1	uptempo
Funny face, Mickey (Bar), Nikki (M)	B♭-b♭/b♭-d2	moving ballad
My one and only reprise, Billy	d-d1	uptempo
Kickin' the clouds away, Montgomery (Bar)	d-d1	uptempo
How long has this been going on?, Edythe, Billy incidental	a-b1	ballad

The Mystery of Edwin Drood (1987)
Music and Lyrics by Rupert Holmes

Song title, **Character (Voice)**	**Range**	**Song Style**
There you are, company		mod. uptempo
Two kinsmen, Drood (M), Jasper (T)	b-d2/e-f1	uptempo
Moonfall, Rosa (S)	b-g2	ballad
The wages of sin, Puffer (M)	g♭-c2	moving ballad
A British subject, ensemble		tango ballad
Both sides of the coin, Jasper, Chairman (Bar)	d#-e2/d-f#1	mod. uptempo
Perfect strangers, Drood, Rosa	c#1-d#2/c#1-f2	mod. ballad
No good can come from bad, ensemble		mod., patter
Never the luck, Bazzard (T)	c-b♭	waltz ballad
Off to the races, Chairman, Durdles (Bar), Deputy (T), company	c-f1/c-d1/c-f1	mod. uptempo
England reigns, Chairman	c-c1	anthem ballad
A private investigation, Datchery (M or Bar), Puffer	A♭-d♭1/a♭-d♭2	mysterious, narrative ballad
The name of love/Moonfall reprise, Rosa, Jasper, company	d1-b2/d-g1	uptempo/ballad
Don't quit while you're ahead, company		soft shoe ballad
The garden path to hell, Puffer	g-a1	mod. ballad
Puffer's revelation, Puffer	a-b♭1	quick, agitated
Out on a limerick, Datchery, company	a-c#2 if woman, c-e1 if man	mod. ballad or uptempo
Jasper's confession, Jasper	b-a1	hard ballad
*Murderer's confession**		mod. uptempo
Helena	g-b1	
Bazzard	a-b♭1	
Neville	e-f1	
Crisparkle	d-f1	
Rosa	a-a♭2	
Puffer	f-c2	
Durdles	c-e1	
*Perfect strangers reprise**		moving ballad
Rosa or Helena or Puffer, with	c#1-e2	
Durdles or Sapsea or Jasper; company	c#-e1	
The writing on the wall, Drood, company	g-e2	uptempo

*Only one character or duo sings these numbers, depending upon who is named by the audience as the murderer.

Naughty Marietta (1910)

Music by Victor Herbert   Lyrics by Rida Johnson Young

Song title, Character (Voice)	Range	Song Style
Come, for the morn is breaking, chorus		uptempo
Tramp, tramp, tramp, Capt. Dick (T), men's chorus	g-c2	character march
Taisez vous, chorus		uptempo
Naughty Marietta, Marietta (S)	b-a2	uptempo
It never, never can be love, Marietta, Capt. Dick	e1-g#2/e-f#1	ballad
If I were anybody else but me, Lizette (S), Simon (Bar)	c1-f2/B♭-f1	ballad, funny
'Neath the Southern moon, Adah (M)	g#-f2	mod. ballad
Italian street song, Marietta, chorus	e1-c3	character
Oh, la, papa!, company		uptempo
You marry a marionette, Etienne (Bar)	F-d1	character, mod.
New Orleans jeunesse dorée, men's chorus		uptempo
Lovers of New Orleans, chorus		uptempo
The sweet by and by, Lizette	c1-c2	ballad
Live for today, Marietta, Adah, Capt. Dick, Etienne	SATB	moving ballad
I'm falling in love with someone, Capt. Dick	e♭-b♭1	waltz ballad
It's pretty soft for Simon, Simon	e-g#1	mod. character
Ah, sweet mystery of life, Marietta, Capt. Dick, company	c#1-a2/e-a1	uptempo

New Girl in Town (1957)

Music and Lyrics by Robert Merrill

Song title, Character (Voice)	Range	Song Style
Roll your socks up, company		uptempo
Anna Lilla, Chris (Bar)	c-c1	folksy ballad
Sunshine girl, Larry (Bar), Oscar (T), Pete (T)*	d#-c1/d#-f1/d#-a1	mod. uptempo
On the town, Anna (M)	e-a2	angry uptempo
Flings, Marthy (S), Lily (S), Pearl (S)	g1-b2/g1-b2/g1-a2	mod. ballad, funny
It's good to be alive, Anna	e-b♭1	ballad
Look at 'er, Matt (Bar)	B♭-f1	mod. ballad

It's good to be alive reprise, Matt	A#-e1	ballad
Yer my freind, Marthy, Chris	d1-a2/d-f1	mod. ballad
Did you close your eyes?, Matt, Anna	B♭-g1/a-e♭2	ballad
Check apron ball, company		mod. uptempo
There ain't no flies on me, Alderman (Bar), Town Politician (Bar), Larry, chorus	all d-e1	uptempo, then soft shoe, then jelly roll
Ven I valse, Chris, Anna, chorus	B-e1/g-e♭2	flowing waltz
Sunshine girl reprise, chorus		mod. uptempo
If that was love, Anna	a♭-a♭1	ballad
Seaman's home, Marthy, chorus (many soli)	b♭-a2	mod. ballad
Bows: Sunshine girl, company		uptempo

* "Barbershop" trio.

The New Moon (1928)
Music by Sigmund Romberg
Lyrics by Oscar Hammerstein II, Frank Mandel, and Laurence Schwab

Song title, Character (Voice)	Range	Song Style
Dainty wisp of thistledown, chorus		march uptempo
Marianne, Robert (Bar)	b♭-e♭1	moving ballad
Marianne, we want to love you, Marianne (S), men's chorus	g1-a2 (opt. c2)	uptempo
The girl on the prow, Marianne, Besac (Bar)	a-g2 (opt. b♭2)/d-d1	mod. uptempo
Gorgeous Alexander, Julie (M), Alexander (Bar), women's chorus	c#1-d2/c#-d1	mod. uptempo
I'm seeking the hand of a maiden, Duval (Bar), Marianne	d-e1/d1-e2	ballad
Red wine in your glasses, chorus		uptempo waltz
Softly as a morning sunrise, Philippe (T), chorus	f-c2	ballad
Stouthearted men, Robert, Philippe, men's chorus	d-f#1 (opt. g1)/d-d1	march
Fair Maria, Marianne, women's chorus	f1-f2	uptempo tango
One kiss, Marianne, women's chorus	e♭1-b♭2	ballad
The trial, ensemble		mod. uptempo
Gentle airs, courtly manners, chorus		mod. ballad
Wanting you, Marianne, Robert	b♭-b♭2/B♭-f1 (opt. g1)	waltz ballad
Funny little sailormen, Clotilde (M), Besac	c1-e2/d-f1	fast character

Lover, come back to me, Marianne	d1-g2	ballad
Stouthearted men reprise, men's		march
chorus		
Love is quite a simple thing, Julie,	SATB	mod. ballad
Alexander, Besac, Clotilde		
Just one year ago we were mated,		moving ballad
chorus		
Softly . . . morning sunrise reprise,	f-c2	ballad
Philippe, men		
Never for you, Marianne	f#1-ab2	ballad
Lover, come back to me reprise, Robert,	d-d1	ballad
Marianne incidental		
One kiss reprise, Robert, Marianne	d-eb1/d1-bb2	ballad
Finale: Stouthearted men, company		march uptempo

Nine (1982)

Music and Lyrics by Maury Yeston

Song title, **Character (Voice)**	**Range**	**Song Style**
Not since Chaplin, chorus		uptempo
Guido's song, Guido (Bar), women's	A-g1	uptempo
chorus		
The Germans at the spa, Mama (M),	g-e2	fast character
chorus		
My husband makes movies, Luisa (M)	eb-c2	moving ballad
A call from the Vatican, Carla (S)	a-c3	mod. uptempo
Only with you, Guido	G#-d1	moving ballad
The script, Guido	d-f1	uptempo
Follies bergeres, La Fleur (M), Critic	g#-b1/B-b	mod. uptempo
(Bar), chorus		
Nine, Mama, Aunts	c1-a2	moving ballad
Be Italian, Saraghina (M), men's chorus	g#-db2	ballad
The bells of St. Sebastian, Guido,	e-g1	moving ballad
chorus		
Unusual way, Claudia (M), Guido	c#1-e2/G#-c#1	ballad
Contini submits/Grand canal, Guido,	d-g1	uptempo, patter
chorus*		ending
Every girl in Venice, Spa Lady (M),	g1-e2	moderate
women's chorus		
Amor, Guido, women's chorus	f-g1	ballad
Only with you, Guido, Nun's ensemble	c-e1	moving ballad
Simple, Carla	a-e2	ballad
Be on your own, Luisa	g#-a1	ballad

I can't make this movie, Guido	g-g1†	mod., driving
Getting tall, Boy (boy S)	a♭-e♭2	ballad
Finale: Nine reprise/Long ago, company		uptempo

*Chorus sings only on "Grand Canal."
† Song also provided in E minor (one step higher) and B-flat (a half-step lower).

No, No, Nanette (1925)

Music by Vincent Youmans   Lyrics by Irving Caesar and Otto Harbach

Song title, **Character (Voice)**	**Range**	**Song Style**
Too many rings around Rosie, Lucille (M), men's chorus	b-d2	ragtime ballad
I've confessed to the breeze, Nanette (S), Tom (T)	b-f2/d-f1	ballad
The call of the sea, Billy (T)	c#-f#2	uptempo
I want to be happy, Nanette, Jimmy (T), men	c1-e2/d-f#1	mod. uptempo
No, no, Nanette, Nanette, men	c1-e♭2	uptempo
You can dance with any girl, Tom, Nanette, chorus	c-e♭1/b♭-d2	uptempo
Peach on the beach, Nanette, company	b-e2	uptempo
Tea for two, Tom	e♭-f1	soft shoe ballad
You can dance with any girl at all, Lucille, Billy	a-e♭2/c-f1	mod. uptempo
What a peach of a girl, company		mostly uptempo
Telephone girlie, Billy, SSA trio	c-f1	uptempo
Where-has-my-hubby-gone blues, Lucille, men	g-d♭2	blues ballad
Waiting for you, Nanette, Tom	a♭-e♭2/B♭-f1	moving ballad
Take a little one-step, Sue (M), company	g-a♭1	uptempo
I want to be happy reprise, company		uptempo
Tea for two reprise, company		soft shoe ballad

No Strings (1962)
Music and Lyrics by Richard Rodgers

Song title, **Character (Voice)**	**Range**	**Song Style**
The sweetest sounds, Barbara (M), David (Bar)	a-d2/f-e♭1	ballad
How sad, David	d-e1	uptempo
The sweetest sounds reprise, David	d-d1	ballad
Loads of love, Barbara	a-b♭1	swing ballad
The man who has everything, Gregg (Bar)	d-d1	uptempo
Be my host, company		uptempo
La-la-la, Jeanette (M), Luc (Bar)*	b-c#2/e-d1	soft shoe ballad
You don't tell me, Barbara	a♭-c2	uptempo
Love makes the world go round, Comfort (M), Mollie (M)	both a-d♭2	waltz ballad
Nobody told me, David, Barbara	d-e♭1/a-a#1	ballad
Look no further, Barbara, David	a-b♭1/B♭-b♭	uptempo
Maine, David, Barbara	d-e♭1/b-c2	moving ballad
An orthodox fool, Barbara	a-c2	uptempo
Eager beaver, Comfort, Mike (Bar)	c1-e2/c-e1	uptempo
No strings, David, Barbara	c#-d1/b♭-c2	moving ballad
Maine reprise, David, Barbara	B♭-a♭1/b♭-a♭2	ballad (slower this time)
The sweetest sounds reprise, David, Barbara	e-d1/c1-g1	ballad
No strings reprise, company		mod. uptempo

*In French.

Nunsense (1985)
Music and Lyrics by Dan Goggin

Song title, **Character (Voice)**	**Range**	**Song Style**
Nunsense is habit forming, company		mod. uptempo
A difficult transition, company		uptempo
Benedicite, Sr. Mary Leo (S)	c#1-g2	mod. uptempo
The biggest ain't the best, Sr. Mary Hubert (M), Sr. Mary Leo	g-f#2/a-a1	moving ballad
Playing second fiddle, Sr. Robert Anne (M)	b-b1	uptempo
So you want to be a nun, Sr. Mary Amnesia (S)	c1-b2	uptempo

Song title, Character (Voice)	Range	Song Style
One last hope, company		uptempo
Turn up the spotlight, Sr. Mary Cardelia (M)	b-f1	uptempo
Lilacs bring back memories, Cardelia, Hubert, Leo, Amnesia	SSAA	ballad
Tackle that temptation with a time step, company		uptempo
Growing up Catholic, Robert Anne, Leo, Hubert, Amnesia	SSAA	moving ballad
We've got to clean out the freezer, company		uptempo
Just a coupl'a sisters, Cardelia, Hubert	both a-c2	jaunty ballad
Playing second fiddle reprise, Robert Anne	d1-b1	moving ballad
I just want to be a star, Robert Anne	g-c2	moving ballad
The drive in, Robert Anne, Amnesia, Leo	e♭-c2/g-c2/b♭-e2	50s ballad
I could've gone to Nashville, Amnesia	g-e2	country ballad
Holier than thou, Hubert, company	b♭-f2	uptempo gospel
Nunsense is habit forming reprise, company		uptempo

Of Thee I Sing (1932)

Music by George Gershwin

Lyrics by Ira Gershwin

Song title, Character (Voice)	Range	Song Style
Wintergreen for president, chorus		uptempo
Who is the lucky girl to be?/Because, because, chorus		uptempo
How beautiful, Diana (S), chorus	d1-f2	character
Love is sweeping the country, Miss Benson (S)	c1-f2	uptempo
Of thee I sing, Mary (S), Wintergreen (Bar)	d1-e2/d-e1	uptempo
Hello, good morning, chorus		mod. uptempo
Who cares?, Mary, Wintergreen, Reporters	d1-e♭2/d-e♭1	ballad
The illegitimate daughter, French Ambassador (Bar), company	d-e1	mod. uptempo
The senator from Minnesota, men's chorus		mod. ballad
The senate, Diana, Fr. Ambassador, men's chorus	d1-f#2/d-d1	uptempo

Prosperity is just around the corner, company		uptempo
Trumpeter blow your golden horn, chorus		uptempo
Of thee I sing reprise, company		uptempo

Oh, Kay! (1926)

Music by George Gershwin   Lyrics by Ira Gershwin

Song title, **Character (Voice)**	**Range**	**Song Style**
The woman's touch, women's chorus		uptempo
Don't ask, Potter (T); Dolly (S), Phillipa (S), women's chorus incidental	d-g1	mod. uptempo
Dear little girl, Jimmy (T)	e♭-e♭1	mod. ballad
Maybe, Jimmy, Kay (S)	c-f1/c1-f2	ballad
Clap yo' hands, Potter, company	c-d1	mod. uptempo
Do-do-do, Jimmy, Kay	d-f1/d1-f2	mod. ballad
Isn't it grand, chorus		uptempo
Never too late to Mendelssohn, company		uptempo
Someone to watch over me, Kay	e♭1-f2	ballad
Fidgety feet, Potter, Phillipa incidental	e♭-f1	mod. uptempo
Heaven on earth, Jimmy, women's chorus	e♭-g1	mod. uptempo
Someone to watch over me reprise, unison chorus		ballad
Maybe reprise, unison chorus		ballad
Oh, Kay!, Kay, men's chorus	e♭1-f2	uptempo
Finale: Do-do-do/Clap yo' hands, company		mod. ballad/ uptempo

Oklahoma (1943)

Music by Richard Rodgers   Lyrics by Oscar Hammerstein II

Song title, **Character (Voice)**	**Range**	**Song Style**
Oh, what a beautiful morning, Curley (Bar)	d#-d#1	ballad
The surrey with the fringe on top, Curley	d#-e1	mod. ballad
Kansas City, Will (T)	e♭-f1	mod. uptempo
I cain't say no, Ado Annie (S)	c1-e2	fast character

Song title, Character (Voice)	Range	Song Style
Many a new day, Laurey (S)	d1-e2	mod. ballad
People will say we're in love, Curley, Laurey	d-f#1/d1-f#2	ballad
Pore Jud is dead, Curley, Jud (Bar)	both d-c#1	narrative ballad
Lonely room, Jud	d-c#1	ballad
Out of my dreams, Laurey, women's chorus	e1-f2	moving ballad
The farmer and the cowman, Old Man Carnes (T), Aunt Eller (M), chorus	f-f1/g-f2	fast character
All 'er nothin',' Annie, Will	eb1-eb2/e-f1	character ballad
People will say . . . reprise, Curley, Laurey	d-f#1/d1-f#2	ballad
Oklahoma, company		uptempo
Finale: Beautiful morning/People will say, company		ballads

Oliver! (1963)
Music and Lyrics by Lionel Bart

Song title, Character (Voice)	Range	Song Style
Food, glorious food, boy's chorus		uptempo
Oliver, Mr. Bumble (T), Widow Corney (M), chorus		mod. uptempo
I shall scream, Widow Corney, Mr. Bumble	db-db1/db-f2	fast character
Boy for sale, Mr. Bumble	d-a1	ballad
That's your funeral, Mr. Sowerberry (Bar), Mrs. Sowerberry (M), Mr. Bumble	c-e1/c1-c2/c-f1	uptempo
Where is love?, Oliver (boy S)	c1-d2	ballad
Consider yourself, The Artful Dodger (boy T), Oliver, unison boy's chorus	b-c#2/a-b1	mod. uptempo
Pick a pocket or two, Fagin (Bar), boys	c-db1	fast character
It's a fine life, ensemble	MMTTB	mod. uptempo
Be back soon, Fagin, boys	c-d1	uptempo
Oom-pah-pah, Nancy (M), chorus	a-b1	fast character
My name, Bill Sykes (Bar)	d-d1	menacing ballad
As long as he needs me, Nancy	f-bb1	ballad
Who will buy?, company		uptempo
Reviewing the situation, Fagin	c-f1	moving ballad
Oliver reprise, Mr. Bumble, Widow Corney	d-f1/d1-f2	mod. uptempo
As long as he needs me reprise, Nancy	bb-c2	ballad

Finale: Food/Consider yourself/I'd do   uptempo/mod.
   anything, company   ballad

On a Clear Day You Can See Forever (1965)

Music by Berton Lane   Lyrics by Alan Jay Lerner

Song title, **Character (Voice)**	**Range**	**Song Style**
On a clear day, chorus		mod. uptempo
Hurry! It's lovely up here!, Daisy (M)	a♭-d♭2	character
Solicitor's song, quartet	TTBB	fast character
He wasn't you, Daisy	g-c2	ballad
On a clear day reprise, Mark (Bar)	A#-e1	moving ballad
On the S. S. Bernard Cohn, Daisy, chorus	d#-d2	uptempo
She wasn't you, Edward (T), Daisy incidental	c-a♭1	ballad
Melinda, Mark	A#-d#1	ballad
When I come around again, company		uptempo
What did I have that I don't have?, Daisy	a♭-c2	ballad
Wait till we're sixty-five, Warren (T), Daisy, students	c-f1/c1-e2	uptempo
Come back to me, Mark	d-e1	uptempo
Finale: On a clear day, company		mod. uptempo

On the Town (1944)

Music by Leonard Bernstein   Lyrics by Betty Comden and Adolph Green

Song title, **Character (Voice)**	**Range**	**Song Style**
I feel like I'm not out of bed yet, men's chorus		moving ballad
New York, New York, Gabey (T), Chip (T), Ozzie (T)	all c-g1	uptempo
Come up to my place, Chip, Hildy (M)	B♭-g1/d1-d2	uptempo patter
Carried away, Claire (M), Ozzie	F-a1/f-c2	moving ballad
Lonely town, Gabey, chorus	d-a1	ballad
Carnegie Hall pavane, Ivy (M), Dilly (M), chorus	both c1-e♭2	mod. ballad
I can cook, too, Hildy	a-c#2	hot uptempo
Lucky to be me, Gabey	B♭-a1	mod. ballad
So long, baby, unison women's chorus		uptempo
I wish I was dead, Diana Dream (M)	c1-d2	blues ballad

Ya got me, Hildy, Ozzie, Claire, Chip	MMTT	mod. uptempo
I understand, Pitkin (Bar)	A-d1	narrative ballad
Some other time, Claire, Hildy, Ozzie, Chip	MMTT	uptempo
Finale: New York, New York, company		uptempo

On the Twentieth Century (1978)
Music by Cy Coleman   Lyrics by Betty Comden and Adolph Green

Song title, Character (Voice)	Range	Song Style
Stranded, chorus		uptempo
Saddle on the horse, company		uptempo
I rise again, Oscar (T), Oliver (T), Owen (T)	B-e1/others g#-e1	slow waltz
Indian maiden's lament, Imelda (S), girl (S)	e1-f2/c1-a2	character ballad
Veronique, Lily (S); Oscar, chorus incidental	e-g♭1	character ballad
I have written a play, Conductor (Bar)	c-f1	uptempo
Together, Oscar, chorus	c#-e1	uptempo
Never, Lily	b♭-f2	uptempo
Our private world, Oscar, Lily	A-e1/a-e2	moving ballad
Repent, Letitia (S)	e1-f#2	mod. uptempo
Mine, Oscar, Bruce (T)	A-e1/A#-f#1	mod. ballad
I've got it all, Lily, Oscar	b-e2/B-e1	mod. uptempo
I have written a play reprise, Congressman (T)	d-f1	uptempo, funny
Five zeros, Oscar, Owen, Letitia	B♭-a♭1/a♭-d♭2/A♭-e♭1	mod. uptempo
I have written a play, Doctor (Bar)	c-e♭1	uptempo
Sign, Lily, sign, Lily, ensemble	b-f2	uptempo
She's a nut, company		uptempo
Max Jacobs, Max (Bar)	B♭-e♭1	moderate
Babette, Lily, chorus	f#-g2	ballad
Last will and testament, Oscar	B♭-f1	slow, recit.-like
Lily-Oscar, Lily, Oscar	g#1-g#2/c#-e1	ballad
Life is like a train, company		mod. uptempo

On Your Toes (1936)

Music by Richard Rodgers　　　　　　　　Lyrics by Lorenz Hart

Song title, Character (Voice)	Range	Song Style
Two-a-day for Keith, Pa (Bar), Ma (M), Junior (Bar)	men: c-c1/her: c1-c2	uptempo
Questions and answers, Junior, chorus	c-d1	fast character
It's got to be love, Frankie (M), Junior, chorus	d1-d2/d-d1	moving ballad
Too good for the average man, Sergei (Bar), Peggy (M)	both g-a1	ballad, funny
There's a small hotel, Frankie, Junior	b-d2/B-d1	ballad
The heart is quicker than the eye, Peggy, Junior	a-a1/d-e♭1	uptempo
Glad to be unhappy, Frankie	c1-d2	ballad
Quiet night, Hank (Bar), chorus	c-e1	ballad
On your toes, Frankie, chorus	a-c2	uptempo
Quiet night reprise, Sergei, chorus	A-c#1	ballad

Once on This Island (1990)

Music by Stephen Flaherty　　　　　　　Lyrics by Lynn Ahrens

Song title, Character (Voice)	Range	Song Style
We dance, company		uptempo
One small girl, Mama (M), Tonton (Bar), Storytellers	b♭-b1/A-c1	narrative ballad
Waiting for life, Ti Moune (S)	c#1-e2	uptempo
And the gods heard her prayer, company		mod. ballad
Rain, Agwe (T)	f-d#1	mod. samba
Pray, company		uptempo
Forever yours, Ti Moune, Daniel (T), Papa Ge (T), chorus	a#-c#2/e#-f#1/c#-g1	ballad, then faster
The sad tale of the Beauxhommes, company	mostly spoken	mod. uptempo
Ti Moune, Mama, Tonton, Ti Moune	g♭-b♭1/g-e♭1/a-c2	mod. ballad
Mama will provide, Asaka (M), chorus	b-e2	bright calypso
Some say, company		mod. ballad
The human heart, Erzulie (M)	b-c#2	mod. ballad
Pray reprise, company		uptempo
Some girls, Daniel	B-e1	ballad

Song title, Character (Voice)	Range	Song Style
Promises/Forever yours reprise, Papa Ge, Erzulie	c#-g1/c1-d2	ballad
A part of us, Mama, Ti Moune, Tonton	b-b1/b-b1/B-b	ballad
Why we tell the story, company		mod. uptempo, narrative

Once Upon a Mattress (1959)

Music by Mary Rodgers

Lyrics by Marshall Barer

Song title, Character (Voice)	Range	Song Style
Many moons ago, Minstrel (T)	d-g1	narrative ballad
Opening for a princess, company		uptempo
In a little while, Harry (T), Larken (S)	d♭-f1/d♭1-f2	ballad
Shy, Winnifred (M), chorus	b-c#2	mod. character
The minstrel, the jester, and I, Minstrel, Jester (T), King (Bar)	all e-f#1	uptempo, funny
Sensitivity, Queen (M), Wizard (Bar) incidental, women's chorus	a-b1	character; in 5/4
The swamps of home, Winnifred, women's chorus	b♭-f2	ballad
Normandy, Minstrel, Jester, Larken	d-g1/d-b♭1/d1-g2	uptempo
Song of love, Dauntless (Bar); Winnifred, chorus incidental	B-e♭1	uptempo
Quiet, quiet, the Queen insists on quiet, chorus	spoken, with clapping	uptempo
Happily ever after, Winnifred	a♭-c♭2	fast character
Man to man talk, Dauntless, King	e-e1/mute	ballad
Very soft shoes, Jester	d-f1	ballad
Yesterday I loved you, Harry, Larken	c-g1/d-e♭2	ballad
How did she stay awake, company		mod. uptempo

110 in the Shade (1963)

Music by Harvey Schmidt

Lyrics by Tom Jones

Song title, Character (Voice)	Range	Song Style
Gonna be another hot day, company		mod. ballad
Lizzie's comin' home, Jim (Bar), Noah (Bar), chorus	both B-e1	uptempo
Love, don't turn away, Lizzie (S)	d1-f2	ballad
Poker polka, Jim, Noah, HC (Bar), File (T)	TTBB	fast character

The hungry men, chorus		uptempo
Rain song, Starbuck (T), chorus	e♭-a♭1	uptempo
You're not foolin' me, Starbuck, Lizzie	d-e♭1/e♭1-e♭2	ballad
Raunchy, Lizzie, HC incidental	g-g♭2	blues uptempo
A man and a woman, File, Lizzie	c-d1/d1-g2	ballad
Old maid, Lizzie	b-g2	uptempo
Everything beautiful happens at night, chorus		ballad
Melisande, Starbuck	G-g1	uptempo
Simple little things, Lizzie; Starbuck incidental	b-e2	ballad
Little red hat, Jim, Snookie (M)	c-f1/c1-e2	character ballad
Is it really me?, Lizzie, Starbuck	a-e2/B♭-e1	ballad
Wonderful music, Starbuck, File, Lizzie	men: d♭-f1/her: f1-e♭2	ballad
Finale : Rain song reprise, company		uptempo

Pacific Overtures (1976)
Music and Lyrics by Stephen Sondheim

Song title, **Character (Voice)**	**Range**	**Song Style**
The advantage of floating in the middle of the sea, Reciter (Bar), company	B-e♭1	mod. ballad
There is no other way, Observers (T, Bar)	e-g1/e-b	ballad
Four black dragons, Fisherman (T), Thief (Bar); chorus and Reciter incidental	c#-f#1/B-d1	narrative ballad
Chrysanthemum tea, ensemble		mod. uptempo
Poems, Kayama (T), Manjiro (S)	e♭-g1/d1-f2	ballad
Welcome to the Kanagawa, Madam, women's chorus	c1-e2	fast character
Someone in a tree, Old Man (T), Reciter, Boy (T), Warrior (T)	TTTB	uptempo
Please hello, ensemble	TTBBBB	fast character
A bowler hat, Kayama (M)	g-e♭1	narrative ballad
Pretty lady, Three British Soldiers (TBB)	I, III: G-f1/II: F-f1	ballad
Next, company		uptempo

Paint Your Wagon (1951)

Music by Frederick Loewe   Lyrics by Alan Jay Lerner

Song title, Character (Voice)	Range	Song Style
I'm on my way, men's chorus, many soli		uptempo
Rumson Town, Jake (Bar)	B-b	mod. ballad
What's goin' on here, Jennifer (M)	g#-c2	uptempo
I talk to the trees, Julio (T), Jennifer	c-f#1/g-c2	ballad
They call the wind Maria, Steve (Bar), Miners	c-f1	ballad
I still see Elisa, Ben (Bar)	G-c2	ballad
How can I wait, Jennifer	f-c2	ballad
I'm on my way reprise, ensemble		uptempo
Trio, Elizabeth (S), Sarah (M), Jacob (Bar)	eb1-eb2/bb-eb2/c-e1	prayerful ballad
Rumson Town reprise, Jake	B-b	ballad
Whoop-ti-ay, company		uptempo
Carino mio, Julio	Bb-f1	ballad
There's a coach comin' in, men's chorus		uptempo
Hand me down that can o' beans, Jake, chorus	c-c1	fast character
Another autumn, Julio	eb-f1	ballad
Movin', ensemble		mod. uptempo
All for him, Jennifer	b-b1	waltz ballad
Wand'rin' star, Ben	d-eb1	mod. uptempo
I talk to the trees reprise, Jennifer	g-c#2	ballad
The strike, company		uptempo
Wand'rin' star reprise, Miners		mod. uptempo
Finale: I'm on my way reprise, men's chorus		uptempo

The Pajama Game (1954)

Music and Lyrics by Richard Adler and Jerry Ross

Song title, Character (Voice)	Range	Song Style
Racing with the clock, chorus		uptempo
A new town is a blue town, Sid (T)	db-g1	uptempo
I'm not at all in love, Babe (M), women's chorus	a-b1	uptempo, funny
I'll never be jealous again, Mabel (S), Hines (T)	b-d2/B-f1	uptempo

Hey there, Sid, also a voice on tape	e♭-a♭1	ballad
Her is, chorus		uptempo
Once-a-year day, chorus		uptempo
Her is reprise, chorus		uptempo
Small talk, Sid, Babe	d♭-g♭1/a♭-d♭2	uptempo
There once was a man, Sid, Babe	B-b♭1/b♭-e♭2	uptempo
Slow down, women's chorus		moderate
Hey there reprise, Sid	f-g♭1	ballad
Steam heat, Gladys (M), men's chorus	c1-c2	jazzy uptempo
Hey there reprise, Babe	a-b♭1	ballad
Think of the time I save, Hines, women's chorus	c-c1	mod. uptempo, funny
Hernando's hideaway, Gladys, chorus	b-c2	Latin ballad
Seven and a half cents, Prey (Bar), Babe, chorus	d-e1/d1-f#2	uptempo
There once was a man reprise, Babe, Sid	b-b♭3/d♭-b♭1	uptempo

Pal Joey (1940)

Music by Richard Rodgers   Lyrics by Lorenz Hart

Song title, Character (Voice)	Range	Song Style
A great big town, Joey (Bar)	e♭-f1	uptempo
You musn't kick it around, Joey, Gladys (M)	e♭-e♭1/b♭-c2	uptempo
I could write a book, Joey, Linda (M)	e♭-e♭1/d-d1	mod. uptempo
A great big town reprise, women's chorus		uptempo
That terrific rainbow, Gladys, women's chorus	b♭-b♭1	blues ballad
What is a man?, Joey, Vera (M)	d-e♭1/d1-e♭2	ballad
Happy hunting horn, Joey	a♭-f1	uptempo
Bewitched, Vera	d1-d2	ballad
Pal Joey (What do I care for a dame?), Joey, chorus	d-c1	uptempo
The flower garden of my heart, Louis (T), Gladys	e♭-g1/d1-f#2	ballad
Zip, Melba (M)	f#-g1	ballad
Plant you now, dig you later, Gladys, chorus	d1-d2	fast character
Den of iniquity, Vera, Joey	e♭1-e♭2/e♭-e♭1	uptempo
Do it the hard way, Joey, chorus	c-c1	uptempo
Take him, Linda, Vera	both c1-d2	mod. uptempo

Betwitched reprise, Vera	e1-d2	ballad
I could write a book reprise, Joey	e♭-d♭1	uptempo

Passion (1994)
Music and Lyrics by Stephen Sondheim

Song title, **Character (Voice)**	**Range**	**Song Style**
Happiness, Clara (S), Giorgio (Bar)	b♭-e2/A-d1	ballad
Happiness II, Clara, Giorgio	a-e2/A-d#1	ballad
First letter, Clara, Giorgio	f-e2/A-b*	moving ballad
Second letter, Clara, Giorgio		
Third letter, Clara, Giorgio, Soldiers (men's chorus)	2 solo Sol.: d-d1	
Fourth letter, Clara, Giorgio, Fosca (M)	Fosca: f-d2	
I do not read or think, Fosca, Giorgio incidental	f-d2	narrative ballad
How can I describe her, Giorgio, Fosca, Clara, Soldiers	c-d1/spoken/a♭-d♭2	mod. uptempo
Love that fills every waking moment, Clara, Giorgio	b-e2/a-e1	moving ballad
To speak to me of love, Fosca	a#-c#2	moving ballad
Fifth letter, Fosca, Giorgio, Clara, chorus	a-b/B-d1/b-d2	mod. ballad
I wish I could forget you, Fosca, Giorgio incidental	f-c2	slow ballad
Scene eight, Soldiers quintet	TBBBB	moderate
Flashback I, Colonel, Fosca, Mother, Father, Ludovic	SMTTB	slow ballad
Flashback II, Mistress (M)	g#-f2	mod. ballad
Flashback III, Ludovic (T)	c#-g1	mod. ballad
Flashback IV, Fosca, Colonel, Father, Mother, Ludovic, Mistress, others		ballad
Sunrise letter, Clara, Giorgio	a♭-e2/B♭-g1	mod. uptempo
Is this what you call love, Giorgio	A-f1	uptempo
Forty days, Clara	b♭-e2	mod. waltz
Loving you, Fosca	f#-c2	ballad
Giorgio, I didn't tell you, Clara	b♭-f2	mod. ballad
Christmas music, Torasso (T)	e♭-f1	uptempo, in 1
Scene 13, Clara, Giorgio	a-e2/A#-f1	mod. ballad
No one has ever loved me, Giorgio	B-d1	moving ballad
Finale: Your love will live in me, company		ballad

* Giorgio's and Clara's ranges are given once and apply to these four "Letters."

Peter Pan (1979)

Music by Mark Charlap and Jule Styne
Lyrics by Caròlyn Leigh, Betty Comden, and Adolph Green

Song title, Character (Voice)	Range	Song Style
Tender shepherd, Mrs. Darling (M), Children	SSSM	mod. ballad
Crow, Peter Pan (M)	b♭-b♭1	uptempo
Neverland, Peter Pan	f-b♭1	ballad
I'm flying, Peter Pan, Children	a♭-b♭1	uptempo
Pirate's march, men's chorus		uptempo march
Hook's tango, Hook (T)	d-d1 (mostly spoken)	mod. tango ballad
Wendy, Peter, boys	a♭-g2	mod. uptempo
Tarantella, Hook, Pirates	e-e1 (mostly spoken)	mod. march
Grow up, Peter, boys	a-c2	mod. uptempo
Mysterious lady, Peter, Hook	f-a2/c-d♭1	ballad
Distant melody, Wendy (girl S)	a♭-b♭1	ballad
Captain Hook's waltz, Hook, Pirates	c-f1	quick waltz
Crow reprise, Peter, children	b♭-c2	mod. uptempo
Grow up reprise, company		mod. uptempo

Phantom (1991)

Music and Lyrics by Maury Yeston

Song title, Character (Voice)	Range	Song Style
Melody de Paris, Christine (S), chorus	c#1-a2	waltz ballad
Dressing for the night, company		uptempo
Where in the world, Phantom (T)	G-f1	slow ballad
This place is mine, Carlotta (S)	b♭-b♭2	uptempo
Home, Christine, Phantom	c1-a2/c-e1	moving ballad
Phantom fugue I, Phantom, Christine	e♭-g1/e♭1-g2	moving, vocalization
Phantom fugue II, company		mod. uptempo
You are music, Phantom, Christine	e♭-g1/e♭1-b♭2	ballad
The bistro/Melody de Paris reprise, Carlotta, Christine, chorus	c#1-e2/c#1-b2	uptempo
Who could ever have dreamed up you, Count (Bar), Christine	B♭-e♭1/b♭-e♭2	ballad
This place is mine reprise, Carlotta	d1-d2	mod. uptempo
Titania, Oberon (T), chorus	d-g1	moderate
Without your music, Phantom	c-f#1	mod. ballad

Where in the world reprise, Phantom	B♭-e♭1	mod. uptempo
The story of Eric, Carriere (Bar)	G-a1/e1-g2/e1-	narrative ballad,
(mostly spoken), Balladora (S),	c2	anthem-like
Young Eric (boy), chorus		
My true love, Christine	c1-g2	ballad
My mother bore me, Phantom	c#-f#1	slow ballad
You are my own, Carriere, Young Eric	G-e1/g-e2	ballad

Pins and Needles (1937)
Music and Lyrics by Harold Rome

Song title, Character (Voice)	Range*	Song Style
Sing me a song with social significance	c1-f2	anthem ballad
Room for one (S)	b-c2	character ballad
Cream of mush song (Bar)	c1-e2	waltz ballad
One big union for two (Bar) (M)	B♭-c2/c1-e2	moving ballad
Mene, mene, tekel	c1-d2	character
What good is love	c1-d2	ballad
I'm just nuts about you	c1-d2	fast character
Four little angels of peace	e♭1-e♭2	ballad
Chain store daisy	c1-d2	narrative ballad
Back to work, unison chorus		uptempo
It's better with a union man	d1-e2	fast character
I've got the nerve to be in love	b♭-c2	ballad
Not cricket to picket	b♭-d2	uptempo
Sunday in the park	c1-e2	ballad
When I grow up (The G-man song)	c1-d2	uptempo
(Bar)		
Nobody makes a pass at me (S)	c1-f2	funny ballad
(Sitting on you) Status quo, solo, chorus	a-c2	swing ballad
Doing the reactionary	c1-e♭2	uptempo
We sing America, chorus, many soli		anthem ballad

* All ranges are given as notated in the score. Most numbers lack character names in the scores; when one is listed, that character is indicated here.

Pipe Dream (1955)

Music by Richard Rodgers   Lyrics by Oscar Hammerstein II

Song title, Character (Voice)	Range	Song Style
All kinds of people, Doc (T), Hazel (S)	e♭-e♭1/e♭1-e♭2	uptempo
The tide pool, Hazel, Doc, Mac (T)	c#1-f#2/e-f#1/d-f#1	character
Everybody's got a home but me, Suzy (M)	g-b1	ballad
On a lopsided bus, Mac, male chorus	f-f1	uptempo
Bum's opera, Joe (Bar), chorus	e♭-e♭1	uptempo
On a lopsided bus reprise, chorus		moving ballad
Sweet Thursday, Fauna (M)	c1-f2	uptempo
Suzy is a good thing, Fauna, Suzy	both d♭-d2	ballad
All at once you love her, Esteban (T), Doc, Suzy	e-f#1/A♭-c1/a♭-b♭1	ballad
The happiest house on the block, Fauna, girls	e1-f#2	moving ballad
The party that we're gonna have tomorrow night, company		uptempo
We are a gang of witches, women's chorus		character
Will you marry me?, Suzy, Fauna	both b♭-c2	ballad
Thinkin', Hazel	c#1-e2	mod. ballad
Serenade, Esteban	e-f#1	ballad
All at once . . . reprise, Fauna	a♭-b♭1	ballad
How long?, company		uptempo
The next time it happens, Suzy	a-e2	uptempo
Finale: Lopsided bus reprise, company		uptempo

Pippin (1972)

Music and Lyrics by Stephen Schwartz

Song title, Character (Voice)	Range	Song Style
Magic to do, Leading Player (T), company	e-f#1	uptempo
Corner of the sky, Pippin (T)	e-g1 (c2 in falsetto)	moving ballad
War is a science, Charles (Bar), Pippin, chorus	B♭-e1/g-g1	mod. character
Glory, company		mod. uptempo
Simple joys, Leading Player	e f#1	uptempo

No time at all, Berthe (M), male ensemble	f#-a1	uptempo
With you, Pippin	c-a2	ballad
Spread a little sunshine, Fastrada (M)	a-d2	mod. ballad
Morning glow, Pippin, chorus	db-gb1	anthem ballad
Right track, Leading Player, Pippin	both eb-ab1	jazzy uptempo
Kind of woman, Catherine (M), girls incidental	gb-db2	ballad
Extraordinary, Pippin	c-f1	uptempo
Prayer for a duck, Pippin	d-f#1	slow, funny
Love song, Pippin, Catherine	db-eb1/c1-g2	ballad
I guess I'll miss the man, Catherine	f#-g1	ballad
Finale: Think about your life, company, Pippin	a-g1	fast, driving, then slower

The Pirates of Penzance (1981)

Music by Arthur Sullivan

Lyrics by W. S. Gilbert

Song title, Character (Voice)	Range	Song Style
Pour, o pour the pirate sherry, Samuel (B), chorus	Bb-d	uptempo
When Frederic was a little lad, Ruth (M)	g-bb1	jaunty ballad
Oh, better far to live and die, Pirate King (Bar), Pirates (men's chorus)	B-d1	character
Oh, false one, you have deceived me!, Frederic (T), Ruth	B-g1/a-e2	ballad
Climbing over rocky mountains, Edith (S), Kate (S), women's chorus	bb-f2/eb-f2	uptempo
Oh, is there not one maiden breast, Frederic, Mabel (S), women	f-gb1 (opt. bb1)/ eb1-bb2	ballad
Poor wandering one!, Mabel, women's chorus	eb1-bb2	moving ballad
How beautifully blue the sky, Mabel, Frederic, women's chorus	f#1-b2/d-g1	fast chorus; solos slower
Stay, we must not lose our senses, chorus		uptempo
Hold, monsters!, ensemble		character
I am the very model of a modern major-general, Major General (Bar), Pirates	Bb-c1	character; patter
Oh, men of dark and dismal fate, company		uptempo

Oh, dry the glistening tear, Mabel, women	f1-gb2	ballad
When the foeman bares his steel, company		mod. uptempo
When you had left our pirate fold, Ruth, Frederic, Pirate King	a-f#2/f#-f#1/F#-d#1	uptempo
Away! Away! My heart's on fire, Ruth, Pirate King, Frederic	b-f#2/B-d1/a-a1	uptempo
Stay, Frederic, stay!, Mabel, Frederic	d1-bb2/d-g1	uptempo
When a felon's not engaged in his employment, Sergeant (Bar), men	c-c1	character
With cat-like tread, upon our prey we steal, company, many soli		slow march
Sighing softly to the river, company		uptempo

Note: Ranges taken from score of the operetta.

Plain and Fancy (1955)

Music by Albert Hague

Lyrics by Arnold Horwitt

Song title, Character (Voice)	Range	Song Style
You can't miss it, Dan (T), Ruth (M), chorus	B-c1/ab-c2	uptempo
It wonders me, Katie (S), chorus	bb-bb2	ballad
Plenty of Pennsylvania, Emma (M), chorus	f-bb1	uptempo
Young and foolish, Peter (Bar)	c#-e1	ballad
Why not Katie?, Ezra (Bar), male ensemble	Bb-d1	ballad, then uptempo
Young and foolish reprise, Peter, Katie	d-f1/db1-ab2	ballad
It's a helluva way to run a love affair, Ruth	g-c2	uptempo
This is all very new to me, Hilda (S), girls	b-e2	mod. ballad
Plain we live, Papa Yoder (Bar), Amish men	B-e1 (opt. g1)	mod. anthem ballad
Plain we live reprise, company		mod. ballad
How do you raise a barn, company		uptempo
Follow your heart, Peter, Katie, Hilda	B-f#1/b-f#2/b-g2	ballad
City mouse, country mouse, Emma, girls	f-b1	fast character
I'll show him, Hilda	bb-f2	uptempo, angry

Take your time and take your pick,	g-c2/G-d1/c1-f2	mod. ballad
Ruth, Dan, Hilda		
Finale: It wonders me, company		mod. ballad

Porgy and Bess (1935)

Music by George Gershwin   Lyrics by Dubose Heyward and Ira Gershwin

Song title, **Character (Voice)**	**Range**	**Song Style**
Jasbo Brown blues, scat chorus		mod. uptempo
Summertime, Clara (S)	f#1-f#2	ballad
A woman is a sometime thing, Jake (Bar)	d-d1	mod. uptempo
Here come de honey man, chorus		uptempo
They pass by singin', Porgy (Bar)	B-d1	ballad
Dice scene: Oh little stars, company		uptempo
Gone, gone, gone/Overflow, company		spiritual
My man's gone now, Serena (S)	e1-b2	ballad
Leavin' for the promise' land, Bess (S), chorus	f1-f2	gospel spiritual
It take a long pull to get there, Jake, chorus	e-e1	gospel ballad
I got plenty o' nuttin', Porgy, chorus	B-d1	uptempo
Bess, you is my woman, Porgy, Bess	B-c1/c#1-a#2	ballad
Oh, I can't sit down, chorus		uptempo
I ain't got no shame, chorus		uptempo
It ain't necessarily so, Sporting Life (T), chorus	d-g♭1	uptempo
What you want wid Bess?, Bess, Crown (T)	f#1-a2/f-f1 (opt. g♭)	dramatic ballad
I loves you, Porgy, Bess, Porgy	d1-a2/d♭-d♭1	dramatic ballad
Oh, hev'nly father/Oh, de Lawd shake de heavens/Oh, dere's somebody knockin' at de do', chorus, many soli		mod. to quick
A red headed woman, Crown, chorus	d♭-g♭1	character
There's a boat dat's leavin' soon for New York, Sporting Life	d-b♭1	uptempo
Good mornin', sistuh!, chorus		uptempo
Oh, Bess, oh where's my Bess, Porgy, Serena, Maria (M)	c#-e#1/g#1-g#2/b-c2	ballad
Oh Lawd, I'm on my way, Porgy, chorus	e-e1	uptempo gospel

Note: The music is continuous; the reader may discover additional soli or ensembles to excerpt.

Promises, Promises (1968)

Music by Burt Bacharach   Lyrics by Hal David

Song title, Character (Voice)	Range	Song Style
Half as big as life, Chuck (Bar)	B♭-e♭	mod. uptempo
Grapes of Roth, unison scat chorus		uptempo
Upstairs, Chuck	c-f1	mod. uptempo
You'll think of someone, Fran (M), Chuck	b-a1/b-e1	ballad
It's our little secret, Chuck, Sheldrake (Bar)	B♭-f1/c-e1	uptempo
She likes basketball, Chuck	B-d1	waltz ballad
Knowing when to leave, Fran	a-c2	driving uptempo
Where can you take a girl, Dobitch (Bar), chorus	d-d1	uptempo
Wanting things, Sheldrake	c-d1	ballad
Christmas party/Turkey lurkey time, chorus		uptempo
A fact can be a beautiful thing, Marge (M), Chuck, chorus	a-d2/a-d1	mod. ballad
Whoever you are, I love you, Fran	g-b1	ballad
Christmas day, chorus		mod. uptempo
A young pretty girl like you, Doctor (T), Chuck	b♭-g1/b♭-d1	mod. ballad
I'll never fall in love again, Fran, Chuck	b-b1/c#-d1	moving ballad
Promises, promises, Chuck	A-e1	uptempo
Bows: Christmas party, company		uptempo

Redhead (1959)

Music by Albert Hague   Lyrics by Dorothy Fields

Song title, Character (Voice)	Range	Song Style
The Simpson sisters, chorus		mod. uptempo
The right finger of my left hand, Essie (M)	g-a1	character
Just for once, ensemble		mod. uptempo
I feel very marvelous, Essie	a♭-b♭1	uptempo
Uncle Sam rag, chorus		quick ragtime
'Erbie Fitch's dilemma, Essie	g-b♭1	uptempo
She's not woman enough for me, George (T), Tom (Bar)	c-f1/c-e1	ballad, funny

Behave yourself, Sarah (M), Maude (M)	both a-e2	uptempo
Look who's in love, Tom, Essie	A-c1/a-bb1	ballad
My girl is just woman enough for me, Tom, chorus incidental	c-e1	ballad
Two faces in the dark, chorus		ballad
I'm back in circulation, Tom	B-d1	uptempo
We loves ya, Jimey, chorus		uptempo
Look who's in love reprise, Tom	c-e1	ballad
I'll try, Tom, Essie	A-d1/a-a1	moving ballad
Finale: Look who's in love, company		ballad

The Red Mill (1906)

Music by Victor Herbert   Lyrics by Henry Blossom

Song title, **Character (Voice)**	**Range**	**Song Style**
Opening chorus, chorus		uptempo
Mignonette, Tina (M), women's chorus	d1-f2	uptempo march
You can never tell about a woman, Burgomaster (Bar),Willem (Bar)*	both c-d1	mod. ballad, funny
Whistle it, Tina, Kid (Bar), Con (Bar)*	c1-c2/men c-c1	funny ballad
A widow has ways, Bertha (M)	b-e2	waltz ballad
The isle of our dreams, Capt. Doris (Bar), Gretchen (M)	d-e1/d1-f#2	ballad
Go while the goin' is good, company		mod. ballad
Ensemble, company		uptempo
The day is gone, Gretchen, company	c1-f2	ballad
Why this silence?, chorus		uptempo
The legend of the mill, Bertha, chorus	c1-e2	narrative ballad
Good-a-bye, John, Kid, Con (done w/ accent)	both e-d1	uptempo
I want you to marry me, Tina, chorus incidental	c#1-e2	waltz ballad
Every day is ladies' day with me, Governor (Bar), men's chorus	c-eb1	uptempo march
Because you're you, Berthe, Governor	d1-d2/d-d1	ballad
The streets of New York, Kid, Con	unison, f-f1	waltz ballad
Entrance of wedding guests, chorus		stately ballad
In old New York, company in unison		mod. uptempo

Added Song:

If you love but me, Tina, chorus	b-d2	mod. uptempo

* Either number could also work as a solo; they present two sides of the same story, and would also work well sung as a duet.

The Rink (1984)

Music by John Kander   Lyrics by Fred Ebb

Song title, Character (Voice)	Range	Song Style
Colored lights, Angel (M)	a-c2	ballad
Chief cook and bottle washer, Anna (M)	e♭-b♭1	uptempo
Don't ah ma me, Anna, Angel	f-b♭1/a♭-c2	uptempo
Blue crystal, Dino (T)	A-f#1	mod. ballad
Under the roller coaster ("Familiar things"), Angel	a#-a1	mod. ballad
Not enough magic, ensemble		mod. uptempo
We can make it, Anna	e♭-b♭1	ballad
After all these years, The Wreckers (male sextet)	TTTBBB	fast, easy two
Angel's rink and social center, Angel, Wreckers	g♭-c2	mod. uptempo
What happened to the old days?, Anna, Mrs. Silverman (S), Mrs. Jackson (S)	b♭-c2/b♭-g2/b♭-g2	mod. ballad
Colored lights reprise, Angel	a-c2	ballad
The apple doesn't fall, Anna, Angel	e-c2/e-c2	uptempo, funny
Marry me, Lenny (T)	c#-e1	ballad
We can make it reprise, Anna	d-a1	ballad
Mrs. A, Anna, Angel; Suitors (T, T), Lenny incidental	a♭-c2/b♭-c2/Suitors both B-f#1	uptempo
The rink, Wreckers	all f#-a1 or d#-f1	mod. uptempo
Wallflower, Anna, Angel	f-c2/g-a1	mod. ballad
All the children in a row, Angel, Danny (Bar) incidental	f#-c2/e♭-c1	ballad

The Roar of the Greasepaint – The Smell of the Crowd (1965)

Music and Lyrics by Leslie Bricusse and Anthony Newley

Song title, Character (Voice)	Range	Song Style
Beautiful land, company, many soli		mod. uptempo
A wonderful day like today, Sir (Bar), Cocky (T), Urchins (chorus)	B♭-g1/B♭-e♭1	uptempo
It isn't enough, Cocky, Urchins	A-f1	mod. ballad
Things to remember, Sir, Kid (boy S), Urchins	A-e♭1/a#-c#2	uptempo waltz

Put it in the book, Kid, Urchins	d#1-b1	mod. uptempo
This dream, Cocky	A-f#1	ballad
Where would you be without me, Sir, Cocky	B-f1/c-f1	uptempo
Look at that face, Sir, Kid, Urchins	B-e♭1/f#-d2/c-f1	uptempo
My first love song, Cocky, Girl (M)	c-g1/b♭-f2	mod. ballad
The joker, Cocky	d-g1 (opt. a1)	uptempo
Who can I turn to?, Cocky, Urchins incidental	G♭-g1	moving ballad
A very funny funeral/That's what it is to be young, Urchins		mod. uptempo
What a man, Cocky, Urchins	e-e♭1	uptempo
Feeling good, Negro (T), Urchins incidental	d-a♭1	ballad
Nothing can stop me now, Cocky, Urchins	B♭-g#1	uptempo
Things to remember reprise, Sir	c-d1	moving ballad
My way, Cocky, Sir	c-f1/c-d1	mod. uptempo
Who can I turn to reprise, Sir	G-e1	ballad
Beautiful land reprise, Urchins		mod. uptempo
Sweet beginning, Cocky, Sir, company	c-f#1/d-g#1	mod. uptempo

The Robber Bridegroom (1976)

Music by Alfred Uhry   Lyrics by Robert Waldman

Song title, Character (Voice)	Range	Song Style
Once upon the Natchez Trace, Jamie (T), company	d-g#1	uptempo
Two heads, Big Harp (Bar), Little Harp (T), ensemble	both e-e1	mod. ballad
Steal with style, Jamie, chorus	B-g1	uptempo
Hell among the yearlings, Salome (M)	spoken	square-dance
Rosamund's dream, Rosamund (M), Jamie incidental	b♭-e♭1	ballad
Prickle pear and lilybud, Salome, chorus incidental	b-d2	fast character
Soldier's joy, Salome, chorus	spoken	march tempo
Ain't nothin' up, Rosamund, chorus	c1-e2	ballad
Cluck old hen, chorus	spoken	uptempo
Deeper in the wood, chorus, many soli		ballad
Flop-eared mule, chorus	spoken	mod. uptempo
Marriage is riches, company		moving ballad
Little piece of sugarcane, chorus	humming	slow ballad

Love stolen, Jamie, chorus incidental	c-g1	moving ballad
Poor tied up darlin', Little Harp, Goat (T)	d-g1/g-c2	uptempo
Goodbye, Salome, company		uptempo
Sleepy man, Rosamund, chorus	d1-f2	ballad
Where, oh where, Jamie, company	d-g#1	uptempo
Richmond cotillion, Preacher	spoken	uptempo
Finale/Bows: Goodbye, Salome, company		uptempo

Roberta (1933)

Music by Jerome Kern   Lyrics by Otto Harbach

Song title, **Character (Voice)**	**Range**	**Song Style**
Let's begin, unison male quartet	eb-eb1	uptempo
Madrigal, John (Bar), men's chorus	B#-e1	uptempo
You're devastating, Huck (T)	Bb-f1	ballad
You're devastating reprise, Stephanie (M)	g-d2	ballad
Yesterdays, Minnie (S)	c-g2	ballad
Something bad had to happen, Schwarenka (M)	a-f2	moving ballad
You're devastating reprise, Stephanie	g-d2	ballad
The touch of your hand, Stephanie, Ladislaw (T)	b-c2/e-a1	mod. ballad
I'll be hard to handle, Schwarenka	bb-d2	ballad, funny
Hot spot, Schwarenka	b-c2	mod. character
Smoke gets in your eyes, Stephanie	ab-f2	ballad
Let's begin reprise, Huck, Stephanie	eb-d1/eb1-d2	uptempo
Something bad had to happen reprise, John	G-eb1	moving ballad
Don't ask me not to sing, company		uptempo
The touch of your hand reprise, Stephanie, Ladislaw	b-c2/e-a1	ballad
Finale, company		uptempo

Robin Hood (1891)

Music by Reginald de Koven   Lyrics by Harry B. Smith

Song title, **Character (Voice)**	**Range**	**Song Style**
Holla, holla, company		uptempo
Auctioneer's song, Outlaws, chorus	ABBB	uptempo

Song title, Character (Voice)	Range	Song Style
Milkmaid's song, Annabel (S), Allan a Dale (M), women's chorus	g1-a2/d1-f2	mod. ballad
Come the bowmen in Lincoln Green, Robin (T), Outlaws, chorus	f-g1	uptempo
Though it was within this hour, Robin, Marian (S)	g-g1/g1-b2	ballad
I am the Sheriff of Nottingham, Sheriff (Bar), Sir Guy (T), chorus	c-d1/f#-g1	uptempo
When a peer makes love, Sheriff, Sir Guy, Marian	d-e1/d-a1/e1-bb2	uptempo
Come the bowmen . . . reprise, company		uptempo
Finale act I, company		uptempo
Oh, cherrily sounds the hunter's horn, Outlaws, men's chorus		uptempo
Song of brown October ale, Little John (Bar), men's chorus	eb-eb1	uptempo
Oh promise me, Marian	d1-e2 (opt. g2)	ballad
Tinker's song, Sir Guy, Sheriff, Tinkers (chorus)	unison d-g1	fast character
Oh see the little lambkins play, Robin, Outlaws	TTBBBB	uptempo
Forest song, Marian	f#1-b2 (opt. d3)	ballad
A troubadour sang to his love, Robin, Marian, others incidental	e-a1/bb-bb1	ballad
Let us put him in the stocks, Outlaws		waltz uptempo
Armorer's song, Will Scarlet (B)	G-d1 (opt. D)	mod. uptempo
When a maiden weds, Annabel	d1-g2	light ballad
The legend of the chimes, Allan, chorus	c-f1	narrative ballad
There will come a time, Robin, Marian	eb-bb1/e1-bb2	ballad
When life seems made of pains and pangs, ensemble	SSTBB	uptempo
Country dance, company		uptempo

Romance/Romance (1988)

Music by Keith Herrmann   Lyrics by Barry Harman

Song title, Character (Voice)	Range	Song Style
The little comedy, Alfred (T), Josefine (M)	db-f1/db1-eb2	narrative waltz ballad
Goodbye, Emil, Josefine	bb-f2	mod. bal., funny
It's not too late, Alfred, Josefine	Bb-f1/ab-eb2	mod. ballad
Great news, Alfred, Josefine	f#-f#1/c#1-d#2	uptempo
Oh what a performance, Alfred, Josefine	c-f#1/g-d#2	narrative mod. uptempo

Happy, happy, happy, Alfred	B♭-f#1	ballad
Women of Vienna, Alfred	c#-f#1	moving ballad
Yes, it's love, Josefine	a♭-c2	uptempo waltz
A rustic country inn, Alfred, Josefine	c-f1/a-e2	mod. uptempo
The night it had to end, Josefine	a♭-d♭2	ballad
The little comedy reprise, Alfred, Josefine	d♭-f1/c-c2	waltz ballad
Summer share, company	SATBar	uptempo
Think of the odds, Barb (S), Lenny (T)	b-e♭2/b-g1	uptempo
Let's not talk about it, Sam (T), Barb	b-e1/b-c2	ballad
So glad I married her, company	SATB	mod. uptempo
Small craft warnings, Barb, Lenny	b-b♭1/B-c1	ballad
How did I end up here?, Monica (M)	g-c2	uptempo
Words he doesn't say, Sam	A♭-g♭1	ballad
My love for you, Lenny, Barb	B♭-g1/d-e♭2	ballad, funny
Moonlight passing through a window, Sam	d-f1	ballad
Now, Monica	a-d#2	uptempo
Romantic notions, Sam, company*	A-e♭1	ballad
Romance! Romance!, company		uptempo

Note: The roles of Alfred and Sam and Josefine and Monica are played by the same two people.
*Could be done as a solo.

Rose-Marie (1924)

Music by Rudolph Friml and Herbert Stothart
Lyrics by Otto Harbach and Oscar Hammerstein II

Song title, Character (Voice)	Range	Song Style
Prelude and opening, Emile (T), chorus (some in French)	f#-g1	slow
Hard-boiled Herman, Herman (Bar), women's chorus	B♭-e♭1 (much spoken)	fast character
Rose Marie, Jim (T), Malone (T)	both e♭-g1	ballad
The mounties, Malone, men's chorus	e-f#1 (opt. a1)	uptempo march
Lak jeem, Rose Marie (S), men's chorus	c1-a2	uptempo
Rose Marie reprise, company		ballad
Indian love call, Rose Marie, Jim	c1-a2 (opt. b♭2)/c-f1	ballad
Pretty things, Rose Marie, chorus	d1-b♭2	moving ballad
Why shouldn't we?, Herman, Jane (M)	B-f1/b-f2	ballad
Totem tom-tom, Wanda (M), chorus	f1-f2	character ballad

Pretty things!, Ethel (M), women's chorus	c1-g2	uptempo
Only a kiss, Herman, Jane, Malone	d-f#1/e1-f#2/d-f#1	mostly uptempo
Sextet, Rose Marie, Jim, Hawley, Emil, Ethel, Wanda	SAATTB	ballad
Minuet of the minute, Rose Marie, Herman, chorus	b-g#2/B-f#1	uptempo
Door of my dreams/Bridal finale, Rose Marie, chorus	e1-b♭2	ballad
Indian love song reprise, Jim, Rose Marie, company	c-d1/c1-f2	ballad

The Secret Garden (1991)

Music by Lucy Simon   Lyrcis by Marsha Norman

Song title, Character (Voice)	Range	Song Style
Opening: India, chorus		mod. uptempo
There's a girl/The house upon the hill, chorus		mod. ballad
I heard someone crying, Mary (girl S), Lily (S), Archie (T), chorus	c1-d2/d1-b2/d-e♭1	moving ballad
If I had a fine white horse, Martha (M)	g-d2	narrative ballad
A girl in the valley, Lily, Archie	d1-d2/d-e1	ballad
It's a maze, Mary, Martha, Dickon (T), Ben (Bar)	c♭1-c2/e♭1-c2/c♭-f♭1/e-d1	uptempo
Winter's on the wing, Dickon	f#-f#1	uptempo
Show me the key, Mary, Dickon	c1-c#1/d-f1	mod. ballad
A bit of earth, Archie	d♭-g♭1	dramatic ballad
Storm I, chorus		uptempo
Lily's eyes, Dr. Craven (Bar), Archie	c-f1/c-g1	ballad
Storm II, chorus		uptempo
Round-shouldered man, Colin (boy S), Mary	a-d1/b♭-b♭1	moving ballad
Final storm, company		uptempo
The girl I mean to be, Mary	b♭-c2	ballad
Quartet, Craven, Archie, Rose (M), Lily	c-e♭1/c-a1/c1-d2/c1-a2	mod. ballad
Race you to the top of the morning, Archie	e♭-a♭1	narrative ballad
Wick, Dickon, Mary	f-f#1/b-d2	mod. uptempo
Come to my garden, Lily, Colin	c1-g2/c1-e2	ballad
Come spirit come charm, company		mod. uptempo

Disappear, Craven	c-f1	dramatic ballad
Hold on, Martha	f-b♭1	ballad
Where in the world, Archie	f-f1	uptempo
How could I ever know?, Lily, Archie	b♭-a1/d-f#1	ballad

1776 (1969)
Music and Lyrics by Sherman Edwards

Song title, Character (Voice)	Range	Song Style
For God's sake, John, sit down, Adams (T), Congress (men's chorus)	b♭-e♭1	slow waltz
Piddle, twiddle, Adams	d♭-e♭1	mod. uptempo
The Lees of old Virginia, Lee (T), Franklin (Bar), Adams	c-f#1/c-d1/a-d1	mod. uptempo
But, Mr. Adams, Adams, Franklin, Jefferson (T), Sherman (Bar), Livingston (Bar)	TTBBB	mod. ballad
Yours, yours, yours, Adams, Abigail (S)	d♭-f2/d♭-e♭1	ballad
He plays the violin, Martha (S), Franklin, Adams	b♭-d2/c-a/c-d1	waltz ballad
Cool, cool, considerate men, Dickinson (Bar), men's chorus	B♭-e1	slow ballad
Momma look sharp, Courier (T), two men	all B♭-d♭1	ballad
The egg, company	e♭-a♭1	mod. uptempo
Molasses to rum, Rutledge (T)	e♭1-e♭2	waltz ballad
Compliments, Abigail	c-e1/d-d1/c1-	mod. ballad
Is anybody there?, Adams, Franklin, Jefferson, Thompson (Bar)	d1/e♭-e1	mod. uptempo

She Loves Me (1963)
Music by Jerry Bock   Lyrics by Sheldon Harnick

Song title, Character (Voice)	Range	Song Style
Good morning, good day, company		uptempo, light
Sounds while selling, company		mod. uptempo
Days gone by, Maraczek (Bar)	B♭-c1	mod. ballad
No more candy, Amalia (S)	d♭1-f♭2	ballad
Three letters, Amalia, Georg (T)	d1-e2/d-e1	mod. ballad
Tonight at eight, Georg	d-e1	uptempo
I don't know his name, Amalia, Ms. Ritter (M)	c#1-d#2/f#-d♭2	ballad
Perspective, Sipos (Bar)	A-d1	moving ballad

Goodbye, Georg, company		moderate
Will he like me, Amalia	d1-f#2	ballad
Ilona, Kodaly (T); Sipos, Arpad incidental	d-e1	beguine ballad
I resolve, Ritter	a-bb1	uptempo march
A romantic atmosphere, Waiter (T), customers	c#-b2/spoken	slow character
Tango tragique, Georg	B-g1	tango ballad
Mr. Novak, will you please, Amalia	e1-f2	angry ballad
Dear friend, Amalia	db1-f2	ballad
Try me, Arpad (T)	B-e1	uptempo
Days gone by reprise, Maraczek	B-bb1	ballad
Where's my shoe, Amalia, Georg	e1-g2/f-f1	uptempo waltz
Vanilla ice cream, Amalia	d1-b2	mod. uptempo
She loves me, Georg	eb-f1	uptempo
A trip to the library, Ritter	g-c#2	uptempo bolero
Grand knowing you, Kodaly	d-a1	mod. uptempo
Twelve days to Christmas, chorus		uptempo
Vanilla reprise, Amalia, Georg	d1-e2/d-e1	mod. uptempo

Shenandoah (1975)

Music by Gary Geld

Lyrics by Peter Udell

Song title, **Character (Voice)**	**Range**	**Song Style**
Raise the flag, men's choruses		angry ballad
I've heard it all before, Charlie (Bar)	c-e1	mod. ballad
Pass the cross to me, chorus		ballad
Why am I me?, Boy (S), Gabriel (Bar)	a-d2/Bb-d1	bright ballad
Next to lovin' I like fightin' best, company		uptempo
Over the hill, Jenny (M)	c1-d2	waltz ballad
The pickers are comin', Charlie	Ab-eb1	ballad
Next to lovin' . . . reprise, company		uptempo
Meditation I, Charlie	Bb-f1	narrative ballad
We make a beautiful pair, Anne (M), Jenny	g-c2/g-d2	ballad
Violets and silverbells, Sam (Bar), Jenny, chorus	G-bb/g-bb1	waltz ballad
It's a boy, Charlie	Bb-d1	uptempo
Freedom, Anne, Gabriel	g#-c#2/G#-e1	uptempo
Silverbells reprise, James (Bar), Anne	d-d1/b-d2	ballad
Papa's gonna make it alright, Charlie	A-c1	waltz ballad
The only home I know, Corporal (T), chorus	d-f1	ballad

Papa . . . reprise, Jenny	f#-a1	mod. waltz
Meditation II, Charlie	c-e1	reflective ballad
Pass the cross . . . reprise, company		mod. ballad

Show Boat (1927)

Music by Jerome Kern   Lyrics by Oscar Hammerstein II and P. G. Wodehouse

Song title, **Character (Voice)**	**Range**	**Song Style**
Opening: Cotton Blossom, company		mod. uptempo
Where's the mate for me?, Ravenal (T)	d-f#1	ballad
Make believe, Ravenal, Magnolia (S)	B-e1/c1-f2	ballad
Ol' man river, Joe (B), men's chorus	G-e1	ballad
Can't help lovin' dat man, Julie (S), Queenie (M); chorus, Joe incidental	bb-f2/g-bb1	ballad
Life upon the wicked stage, Ellie (M), women's chorus	bb-f2	uptempo
Queenie's bally-hoo, Queenie	g-c2	character
You are love, Ravenal, Magnolia	d-f1/d1-f2	ballad
At the world's fair, chorus		uptempo
Why do I love you?, Magnolia, Ravenal, chorus	c#1-g2/c#-f#1	ballad
Dahomey, chorus		uptempo
Bill, Julie	c1-d2	mod., funny
Can't help . . . reprise, Magnolia	cb-f2	ballad
After the ball, Magnolia*	d1-f2	ballad
Ol' man river reprise, Joe	G-e1	ballad
You are love reprise, Ravenal	c-ab1	ballad
Finale: Ol' man river, company		ballad

* Turn-of-the-century song by Charles K. Harris, interpolated here.

Silk Stockings (1955)

Music and Lyrics by Cole Porter

Song title, **Character (Voice)**	**Range**	**Song Style**
Too bad, company		mod. uptempo
Paris loves lovers, Canfield (Bar), Ninotchka (M)	Ab-db1/gb-f1	mod. ballad
Stereophonic sound, Janice (M), men's chorus incidental	a-bb1	uptempo

It's a chemical reaction, Ninotchka, Canfield	f#-f2/A-d1	mod. uptempo
Satin and silk, Janice	g-b1	mod. ballad
Without love, Nina (M)	e♭-f1	mod. ballad
Hail Bibinski, company		uptempo
As on the seasons we sail, Canfield, Nina	A-d1/g-g1	moving ballad
Josephine, Janice, chorus	a♭-b♭1	fast character
Siberia, ensemble		uptempo
Silk stockings, Canfield	B♭-d♭1 (opt. f1)	mod. ballad
Stereophonic . . . reprise, Janice, men	a-b♭1	uptempo
Red blues, chorus		blues ballad
Too bad reprise, company		uptempo

Song of Norway (1944)
Music by Edvard Grieg
Musical Adaptation and Lyrics by Robert Wright and George Forrest

Song title, **Character (Voice)**	**Range**	**Song Style**
The legend, Rikaard (T)	e-a♭1	mod. ballad
Hill of dreams, Nina (S), Edvard (Bar), Rikaard	d♭1-b♭2/B♭-f1/e♭-a♭1	mod. uptempo
Freddy and his fiddle, Einar (T), Sigrid (S)	c#-g1/d1-g2	mod. uptempo
Now, Louisa (S), chorus	c1-a♭2	uptempo, then waltz ballad
Strange music, Nina, Edvard	d1-b♭2/B-g1	moving ballad
Midsummer's eve, Rikaard, Louisa	d-g1/d♭1-a2	ballad
March of the Trollgers, company		uptempo
Hymn of betrothal, Mother Grieg (M), Rikaard incidental, chorus	e1-d2	anthem ballad
Now! Now!, company		mostly uptempo
Bon vivant, company		uptempo
Three loves, Louisa, Edvard	c1-a2/B-e♭1	moving ballad
One love alone, chorus		uptempo
Waltz eternal, chorus		uptempo
I love you, Nina	f#1-g2	ballad
At Christmas time, Father Grieg (Bar), Mother Grieg, Nina, ensemble	G-b/b♭-d2/e1-e2	uptempo

The Sound of Music (1959)

Music by Richard Rodgers   Lyrics by Oscar Hammerstein II

Song title, **Character (Voice)**	**Range**	**Song Style**
Dixit Dominus/Alleluia (chant), women's chorus		slow
The sound of music, Maria (S)	b-b1	ballad
Maria, women's ensemble		mod. uptempo
My favorite things, Maria, Mother Abbess incidental	b-e♭2	mod. waltz
Do-re-mi, Maria, Children	c1-g2	uptempo
Sixteen going on seventeen, Liesl (S), Rolf (T)	b-c2/d-e♭1	waltz ballad
The lonely goatherd, Maria, Children	c1-b♭2	fast character
How can love survive?, Max (T), Elsa (M)	d-f1/d1-f2	ballad
The sound of music reprise, Captian (Bar), Children	B-b1	ballad
So long, farewell, Children		mod. uptempo
Nuns' processional/Morning hymn, women's chorus		slow
Climb ev'ry mountain, Mother Abbess (M)	c1-a♭2	anthem ballad
The sound of music reprise, Children		ballad
My favorite things reprise, Children		mod. waltz
No way to stop it, Max, Elsa, Captain	c-e1/c1-b2/c-e1	uptempo
An ordinary couple, Captain, Maria	G-d1/b-d2	ballad
Processional, Nuns		ballad
Canticle: Confitemini Domino, Nuns		ballad
Sixteen going on seventeen reprise, Maria, Liesl	b-c#2/b1-b2	ballad
The concert: Do-re-mi, Trapp family		uptempo
So long, farewell reprise, Family		mod. uptempo
Finale: Climb every mountain, Mother Abbess, Nuns	c1-g2	ballad

South Pacific (1949)

Music by Richard Rodgers   Lyrics by Oscar Hammerstein II

Song title, **Character (Voice)**	**Range**	**Song Style**
Dites-moi, ensemble w/ incidental soli		slow
A cockeyed optimist, Nellie (M)	a-c2	uptempo

Twin soliloquies, Nellie, Emile (Bar)	c1-b1/B-b	ballad
Some enchanted evening, Emile	c-e1	ballad
Bloody Mary, men's chorus		uptempo
There is nothing like a dame, men's chorus		uptempo
Bali ha'i, Mary (M)	g-g1	ballad
Cable hears Bali ha'i, Cable (T)	d-d1	ballad
I'm gonna wash that man right out-a my hair, Nellie, women's chorus	b-b1	fast character
Some enchanted evening reprise, Emile, Nellie	c-e1/c1-f1	ballad
I'm in love with a wonderful guy, Nellie, women	b-c2	uptempo
Bali ha'i reprise, French girls	e-g1	ballad
Younger than springtime, Cable, women incidental		ballad
I'm in love with a wonderful guy reprise, Nellie	c1-c2	uptempo
This is how it feels, Nellie, Emile	bb-d2/Bb-c1	mod. ballad
I'm gonna wash that man . . . reprise, Emile	B-b	fast character
Happy talk, Mary	a-b1	character
Honey bun, Nellie, chorus	bb-f2	fast character
This nearly was mine, Emile	B-d	waltz ballad
Honey bun reprise, chorus		uptempo

Starting Here, Starting Now (1977)

Music by David Shire   Lyrics by Richard Maltby, Jr.

Song title, **Character (Voice)**	**Range**	**Song Style**
I am in love, Woman 1 (S), Woman 2 (M), Man (Bar)	d1-f2/d1-eb2/f-e	mod. ballad
Starting here, starting now, Woman 1, 2, Man	b-d2/b-c2/d-e1	mod. uptempo
I'm a little bit off, Woman 2	ab-eb2	quick ragtime
I may want to remember today, Woman 1, 2	both c1-eb2	uptempo
Beautiful, Woman 1, 2, Man	bb-gb1/bb-f2/Bb-e1	ballad
We can talk to each other, Man	c-eb1	uptempo
Just across the river, Woman 1, 2, Man	c1-f#2/bb-d2/Bb-d1	mod. rock uptempo
Crossword puzzle, Woman 2	c-e2	mod. uptempo

Autumn, Woman 1	b♭-e♭2	ballad
I don't remember Christmas, Man	c-e1	uptempo samba
I don't believe it, Woman 1, 2, Man	c#1-e♭/c#1-d2/c#-e♭1	uptempo
I hear bells, Man; Women (on syllables)	B♭-d1/f1-f2/c1-f2	ballad
I'm going to make you beautiful, Woman 1	b♭-g1	uptempo
Pleased with myself, Woman 1, 2, Man	a♭-c3/f-f2/a♭-f1	mod. uptempo
Hey there, fans, Man	A-d1	uptempo
The girl of the minute, Woman 1, Man	d♭1-e♭2/d♭-e♭1	ballad
Travel, Woman 1, 2, Man	a-c#2/b♭-c#2/A♭-c#1	mod. uptempo
Watching the big parade go by, Woman 1	b♭-d2	mod. uptempo
Flair, Man	A-d1	uptempo
What about today?, Woman 2	b♭-b♭1	hard ballad
One step, Woman 1, 2, Man	b-f2/b-d2/c-f1	mod. uptempo
Song of me, Woman 1	d1-f#2	mod. uptempo
Today is the first day, Women	both d♭1-e♭2	mod. ballad
A new life coming, Woman 1, 2, Man	c1-e2/c1-e2/c-f1	uptempo
Flair reprise, Woman 1, 2, Man	d1-g2/d1-e♭2/d-e1	uptempo

Optional Song:
Barbara, Man	G♭-b♭	ballad

Stop the World — I Want to Get Off (1962)
Music and Lyrics by Leslie Bricusse and Anthony Newley

Song title, **Character (Voice)**	**Range**	**Song Style**
The abc song, chorus		character
I wanna be rich, Little Chap (T), girls	d-g1	uptempo
Typically English, Evie (M), Little Chap, solo M, girls	b-d1/c-d1/b-b1	mod. ballad
Lumbered, Little Chap, incidental girl solo	d-f1	uptempo
Gonna build a mountain, Little Chap, girls	c-f1	uptempo
Glorious Russian, Anya (Bar), chorus	G-a	mod. character
Meilinki meilchik, Little Chap, Anya	e♭-e♭1/g-f1	mod. ballad
Family fugue, Little Chap, Evie, Susan (M), Jane (M)	e♭-e♭1/a-c2/a-d2/a-d2	mod. uptempo

Typische deutsche, Ilse (M)	f#-c2	character ballad
Family fugue reprise, Little Chap, Evie	A♭-g♭1/a♭-d♭2	uptempo
Nag, nag, nag, company		mod. uptempo
All American, Ginnie (M)	a-a1	uptempo
Once in a lifetime, Little Chap, solo M	c-f1/d1-c2	ballad
Mumbo jumbo, Little Chap, chorus	spoken	fast character
Once in a lifetime reprise, Little Chap, chorus	B♭-f1	ballad
Someone nice like you, Evie, Little Chap	a♭-b♭1/c-e♭1	ballad
What kind of fool am I?, Little Chap	a♭-f1	ballad

Street Scene (1947)

Music by Kurt Weill   Lyrics by Langston Hughes and Elmer Rice

Song title, Character (Voice)	Range	Song Style
Ain't it awful, the heat?, ensemble		mod. uptempo
I got a marble and a star, Henry (Bar)	B♭-f1	blues ballad
Get a load of that, Mrs. Jones (M), Mrs. Fiorentino (S), Mrs. Olson (M)	c1-e♭2/g1-g2/a♭-c2	uptempo
When a woman has a baby, Buchanen (T)	d-g♭1	moving ballad
Somehow I never could believe, Mrs. Maurrant (S)	d♭1-g2	ballad
Ice cream sextet	SATTBB	uptempo, funny
Let things be like they always was, Maurrant (Bar)	A-d1	mod. ballad
Wrapped in a ribbon and tied in a bow, ensemble		mod. uptempo
Lonely house, Sam (T)	f-b♭1	ballad
Wouldn't you like to be on Broadway, Easter (Bar)	d-f1	mod. uptempo
What good would the moon be?, Rose (S)	d1-g2	moving ballad
Moon faced, starry eyed, Dick (T), Mae (M)	f-f1/d1-d2	uptempo
Remember that I care, Sam, Rose	f-a1/d1-a2	ballad
Catch me if you can, Children's chorus		uptempo
There'll be trouble, Mrs. Maurrant, Rose, Maurrant	e♭1-a2/d1-g2/A#-f1	angry uptempo
A boy like you, Mrs. Maurrant	g1-g2	mod. ballad
We'll go away together, Rose, Sam	e♭1-g2/e♭-g1 (opt. b♭1)	uptempo

The woman who lived up there, chorus		slow, narrative
Lullaby, two nursemaids (S, M), chorus	c1-g2/a♭-e2	ballad
I loved her too, chorus		ballad
Don't forget the lilac bush, Sam, Rose	e♭-a♭1/d1-g2	ballad

Strike Up the Band (1930)

Music by George Gershwin   Lyrics by Ira Gershwin

Song title, Character (Voice)	Range	Song Style
Fletcher's American cheese choral society, Timothy (T), Sloane (Bar), Fletcher (T), chorus	d♭-e♭1/c- d♭1/d♭-e♭1	uptempo
17 and 21, Timothy, Anne (S)	e♭-e1/e♭1-f2	mod. ballad
Typical self-made American, Fletcher, Jim (Bar), men's chorus	B-e1/e-e1	mod. uptempo
Meadow serenade, Jim, Joan (S)	d-f1/d1-b2	mod. ballad
Unofficial spokesman, Fletcher, Holmes (T), chorus	c-e1/c-e♭1	uptempo
Patriotic rally, chorus		march uptempo
The man I love, Joan, Jim	d1-a2/f-f1	ballad
Yankee doodle rhythm, Spelvin (Bar), chorus	e-e1	uptempo
17 and 21 reprise, Mrs. Draper (S), Fletcher	e♭1-f2/e♭-f1	mod. ballad
He knows mild, company		uptempo
Strike up the band, Timothy, chorus	f-g1	uptempo
Oh this is such a lovely war, chorus		waltz uptempo
Come-look-at-the-war choral society, women's chorus		mod. uptempo
Hoping that someday you'd care, Jim, Joan	d-f1/d1-f2	ballad
Miltary dancing drill, Timothy, Anne, chorus	c-f1/c1-f2	march uptempo
How about a man?, Mrs. Draper, Holmes, Fletcher	e♭1-g2/c- g1/e♭1-a♭2	mod. uptempo
Homeward bound/The girl I love reprise, Soldier (T)	g-b♭1	uptempo/ballad
The war that ended war, chorus		march uptempo
Strike up the band reprise, company		uptempo

Note: Many songs here were added in a later revision.

The Student Prince (1924)

Music by Sigmund Romberg   Lyrics by Dorothy Donnelly

Song title, Character (Voice)	Range	Song Style
Prologue, quartet	TTBB	mod. uptempo
Golden days, Prince (T), Engel (Bar)	c#-g#1/f-eb1	ballad
Garlands bright, women's chorus		mod. uptempo
To the inn we're marching, men's chorus		uptempo
Drinking song, men's chorus		uptempo
Where is the maid?, Kathie (S), chorus	e1-c3	uptempo
Drinking song reprise, men's chorus		uptempo
Heidelberg, beloved vision, chorus		anthem ballad
Gaudeamus, men's chorus		anthem ballad
Golden days reprise, Engel	c-eb1	ballad
Come sir, will you join?, ensemble, men's chorus		uptempo
Overhead the moon is beaming, company		mod. ballad
Farmer Jacob lay a-snoring, men's chorus		mod. character
Student life, company		uptempo
Just we two, Princess (S), Tarnitz (T), men's chorus	d1-g2/d-g1	mod. uptempo
What memories, sweet Rose, company		mod. ballad
Let us sing a song, men's chorus		uptempo
To the inn we're marching reprise, company		uptempo march

Sugar (1972)

Music by Jule Styne   Lyrics by Bob Merrill

Song title, Character (Voice)	Range	Song Style
When you meet a girl in Chicago, Sugar (M), women's chorus	a-c2	uptempo
Turn back the clock, women's chorus		easy ballad
Penniless bums, Joe (Bar), Jerry (Bar), men's chorus	both c-e1	mod. uptempo
Tear the town apart, Spats, men's chorus	spoken	jazzy uptempo
The beauty that drives men mad, Joe, Jerry, chorus	both d-f1	blues ballad

We could be close, Sugar, Jerry	b#-d2/B#-d1	ballad
Sun on my face, ensemble, women's chorus		uptempo
November song, Osgood (Bar), men's chorus	c-d1	easy ballad
Doin' it for Sugar, Joe, Jerry	B-e1/c-e♭1	swing ballad
Hey, why not?, Sugar, men's chorus	b♭-b♭1	mod. uptempo
Beautiful through and through, Osgood; Jerry incidental	c#-e♭1	uptempo waltz
What do you give to a man who's had everything, Joe; Sugar incidental	d-e1	uptempo
Magic nights, Jerry	e-f1	uptempo
It's always love, Joe	c-d1	ballad
When you meet a man in Chicago reprise, company		uptempo

Sugar Babies (1979)
Music by Jimmy McHugh, Arthur Malvin, Jay Livingston, Ray Evens
Lyrics by Arthur Malvin, Dorothy Fields, George Oppenheimer,
Eugene West, Irwin Dash, Jay Livingston, Ray Evens,
Ted Koehler, Jack Frost, Irving Mills

Song title, **Character (Voice)**	**Range**	**Song Style**
Good old burlesque show, Mickey (T), chorus	B-f1	mod. swing
Let me be your sugar baby, women's chorus		uptempo
I feel a song comin' on, Ann (M), chorus	b♭-f1	uptempo
Sally, Production Tenor	c#-g1	uptempo
Immigration Rose, solo T, male quartet	d-f#1	ballad
Don't blame me, Ann	a-a2	mod. uptempo
Sugar baby bounce, Linda (M), Chris (M), Ann	all a♭-e2	ballad
Down at the Gaiety burlesque, women's chorus		uptempo
Mr. Banjo Man, Ann, Mickey, chorus	b♭-b2/B♭-a	uptempo
I'm keepin' myself available for you/ Exactly like you, Ann, women	a-c2	mod. uptempo/ mod. swing
Warm and willing, Rosita Royce (M)	a♭-c2	ballad
Cuban love song, Production Tenor	A-g1	beguine ballad
McHugh medley, Mickey, Ann	B♭-e♭1/f-c#2	mostly uptempo
Uncle Sammy finale, Mickey, Ann, chorus	d-e1/a-e♭2	uptempo

Sunday in the Park with George (1984)

Music and Lyrics by Stephen Sondheim

Song title, **Character (Voice)**	**Range**	**Song Style**
Sunday in the park with George, Dot (M)	e-d♭2	ballad, often funny
No life, Jules (Bar), Yvonne (M)	G-d1/a-d2	ballad
Color and light, Dot, George (T)	b-e2/d-g1	mod. uptempo
Gossip sequence, ensemble		uptempo
The day off, company		mod. uptempo
Everybody loves Louis, Dot	a-c2	uptempo
Finishing the hat, George	B♭-a♭1	uptempo
We do not belong together, Dot, George	g-d2/A-e1	ballad
Beautiful, Old Lady (M), George	f#-b1/c#-f#1	ballad
Sunday, company		moving ballad
It's hot up here, company		mod. uptempo
Putting it together, George, company	d♭-g♭1	uptempo
Children and art, Marie (M), George incidental	g♭-d♭2	moving ballad
Lesson no. 8, George	G♭-f1	ballad
Move on, George, Dot	d#-g1/g#-c#2	moving ballad
Sunday reprise, company		mod. uptempo

Note: The characters of Dot and Marie are played by the same actress.

Sunny (1925)

Music by Jerome Kern   Lyrcis by Otto Harbach and Oscar Hammerstein II

Song title, **Character (Voice)**	**Range**	**Song Style**
Here we are together again, chorus		uptempo
Here you come a-running, Tom (T)	e♭-f1	ballad
Who?, Sunny (S), Tom	b-e2/B-e1	uptempo
So's your old man, Wendell (T), chorus	d-g1	uptempo
Let's say goodnight, Weenie (M), Jim (T)	b♭-e♭2/B♭-e♭1	mod. ballad
D'ye love me, Sunny	b-g2	waltz ballad
It won't mean a thing, Sunny, Tom, Jim, men's chorus	b-a2/B-f1/A-f1	ballad
The wedding knell, Sunny, men's chorus	b-g#2	uptempo
Two little bluebirds, Weenie, Wendell	d1-e♭2/d-e♭1	ballad
Ev'ry guest is in the room, company		uptempo

We're gymnastic, Sue (S), women's chorus	c#1-f2	uptempo
Divorce, Sunny, Jim	b-e2/B-e1	uptempo
Sunshine, Marcia (M), chorus	d1-a2	waltz ballad
The chase, company		mod. uptempo
I might grow fond of you, Weenie, Wendell	c1-e2/c-e1	ballad
The fox has left his lair, unison quartet*	c-f1 (c1-f2)	character
The hunt ball, chorus		mod. uptempo
Who reprise, Jim	d-e1	uptempo
D'ye love me reprise, company		waltz ballad

* Could be performed as a solo.

Sweeney Todd (1979)
Music and Lyrics by Stephen Sondheim

Song title, **Character (Voice)**	**Range**	**Song Style**
No place like London, Todd (B), chorus	G-c#1	mod. uptempo
The worst pies in London, Mrs. Lovett (M)	b-eb2	character
Poor thing, Mrs. Lovett	f#-b1	ballad
My friends, Todd, Mrs. Lovett	Bb-e1/b-eb2	mod. ballad
Green finch and linnet bird, Johanna (S)	c1-g2	uptempo
Johanna, Anthony (T)	c-eb1	ballad
Pirelli's miracle elixir, Tobias (T), chorus	d-ab1	mod. character
The contest, Pirelli (T), chorus	d-c2	mod. uptempo
Johanna, Judge Turpin (Bar)	Bb-f1	angry ballad
Wait, Mrs. Lovett	bb-eb2	ballad
Kiss me I, Johanna, Anthony	c#1-g#2/c#-f#1	flowing ballad
Ladies in their sensitivities, Beadle (T)	d-f#1	character ballad
Kiss me II, Johanna, Anthony, Beadle, Judge	STTB	ballad
Pretty women, Judge, Todd	G-d1/d-e1	mod. ballad
Epiphany, Todd, Mrs. Lovett incidental	c-f1	angry uptempo
A little priest, Mrs. Lovett, Todd	g#-b1/G-gb1	grizzley, mod.
God, that's good, chorus		mod. uptempo
Johanna, Todd, Anthony, Beggar Woman, Johanna	Ab-c/Ab-eb1/ women: ab1-eb2	ballad
By the sea, Mrs. Lovett, Todd	g#-e2/ G#-e1	ballad
The letter, ensemble		mod. ballad
Not while I'm around, Tobias	eb-ab1	ballad

Parlor songs, Beadle, others incidental   d-g1   mod. ballad
City on fire!, chorus   uptempo
Searching, ensemble   mod. ballad
The ballad of Sweeney Todd, company   mod. uptempo

Sweet Charity (1965)

Music by Cy Coleman   Lyrics by Dorothy Fields

Song title, **Character (Voice)**	**Range**	**Song Style**
You should see yourself, Charity (M)	b♭-b♭1	uptempo
Big spender, women's chorus		quick, striptease
Charity's soliloquy, Charity	a♭-a1	mod. uptempo
If my friends could see me now, Charity	g#-b♭1	uptempo, jazzy
Too many tomorrows, Vidal (T)	B♭-g1	40s ballad
There's gotta be something better, Charity, Nikkie, Helene	all a-c#2	driving uptempo
I'm the bravest individual, Charity, Oscar (Bar)	f#-b♭1/c-g1	mod. uptempo
Rhythm of life, Daddy Brubeck (Bar), two assistants, chorus	all d-d1	jazzy chorus
Baby, dream your dream, Nickie, Helene	both f#-c#2	mod. ballad
Sweet Charity, Oscar, chorus incidental	d♭-e1	uptempo
Where am I going?, Charity	g-g1	ballad
I'm a brass band, Charity, men's chorus	a-a1	uptempo march
I love to cry at weddings, Herman (T), company	e-b1 (in falsetto)	uptempo
See me now reprise, company		uptempo

Sweethearts (1913)

Music by Victor Herbert   Lyrics by Robert B. Smith

Song title, **Character (Voice)**	**Range**	**Song Style**
Iron! Iron! Iron!, women's chorus		uptempo
On parade, chorus		uptempo march
There is magic in a smile, Liane (S), chorus	c1-b♭2	ballad
Sweethearts, Sylvia (S), chorus	b♭-b♭2	ballad
Every lover must meet his fate, Prince (T), chorus	c-f1	ballad
Mother Goose, Sylvia, women's chorus	c1-f#2	character ballad

Jeanette and her little wooden shoes, Liane, ensemble	c1-f2	uptempo
The angelus, Sylvia, Prince	f1-a2/c-f1	anthem ballad
The game of love, Karl (T), chorus	e-a2	ballad
May the god of fortune attend you, company		mod. uptempo
Waiting for the bride, double men's chorus		uptempo
Pretty as a picture, Van Tromp (Bar), chorus	B♭-d1	character ballad
What she wanted—and what she got, Paula (M), women's chorus	d1-e2	uptempo, funny
In the convent they never taught me that, Sylvia, chorus incidental	d1-a2	uptempo
Talk about this - talk about that, Liane, Karl	c1-g2/d-g1	moving ballad
I don't know how I do it, but I do, Slingsby (T)	c-e♭1 (mostly spoken)	mod. ballad
The cricket on the hearth, Sylvia, Prince	c#1-f#2/c#-e1	ballad
Pilgrims of love, Slingsby, Van Tromp, Caniche (S)	d-a1/G-c1/d1-f1	march ballad
The ivy and the oak, Sylvia	d1-g2	ballad
Reprises, company *Sweethearts, Indian summer, Pretty as a picture*		uptempo

Take Me Along (1959)
Music and Lyrics by Bob Merrill

Song title, **Character (Voice)**	**Range**	**Song Style**
Opening chorus, Nat (Bar), chorus	spoken	mod. uptempo
Oh, please, Essie (M), Nat, chorus	b♭-e♭2/B♭-e♭1	mod. ballad
I would die, Muriel (M), Richard (T)	b♭-b♭1/c-f1	mod. uptempo
Sid, ol' kid, Sid (Bar), men's chorus	B-f1	fast character
Staying young, Nat	A-d1	mod. uptempo
I get embarrassed, Lily (S), Sid	b♭-f2/F-f	mod. ballad
We're home, Lily	c♭-d♭1	ballad
Take me along, Nat, Sid	both c-c1	uptempo
For sweet charity, Nat, chorus	d♭-f1/f-f1	uptempo
Pleasant beach house, Wint (T)	B-f1	mod. ballad
That's how it starts, Richard	d-a♭1	uptempo
Oh, please reprise, Nat, Essie	B♭-c1/b♭-c2	mod. ballad

Slight detail, Lily	b-d2	mod., funny
Staying young reprise, Nat	A-c1	mod. ballad
Little green snake, Sid	c-eb1	mod. ballad
Nine o'clock, Richard	d-d1	mod. uptempo
But yours, Sid, Lily	Bb-f1/bb-d2	mod. uptempo
Sid, ol' kid reprise, company		uptempo

Tap Dance Kid (1983)

Music by Henry Krieger   Lyrics by Robert Lorick

Song title, Character (Voice)	Range	Song Style
Dipsey's comin' over, Willie (Bar)	G-d1	mod. uptempo
High heels, "Someting better," Dipsey (T)	d-d1	mod. ballad
Four strikes against me, Emma (M)	ab-db1	mod. uptempo
Class act, Dipsey, Ginnie (M), Daddy Bates (Bar)	Bb-g1/bb-eb2/a-d1	big band swing ballad
Four strikes reprise, Emma	c1-db2	mod. uptempo
They never hear what I say, Emma, Willie	bb-d2/c-c1	uptempo
Dancing is everything, Willie	Bb-d1	quick shuffle
Fabulous feet, Dipsey	d-c2	medium shuffle
I could get used to him, Carole (M)	f-e2	ballad
Man in the moon, Dipsey	db-eb1	ballad
Like him, Emma, Ginnie	bb-db2/g-c2	moving ballad
My luck is changing, Dipsey	db-f1	uptempo
Someday, Emma, Willie*	a-d2/A-d1	uptempo
I remember how it was, Ginnie	e-b1	moving ballad
Lullaby, Ginnie	g-g1	ballad
Tap tap, Daddy Bates	db-f1	mod. uptempo
Audition, chorus		mod. 4, shuffle
William's song, William (T)	Bb-gb1	ballad
Class act finale, company		uptempo

*Could be performed as a solo for her.

They're Playing Our Song (1979)

Music by Marvin Hamlisch   Lyrics by Carole Bayer Sager

Song title, **Character (Voice)**	**Range**	**Song Style**
Falling, Vernon (Bar)	A-d1	ballad
Falling reprise, Sonia (M)	e-a1	ballad
Workin' it out, Vernon, Sonia, chorus	eb-gb1/f-bb1	mod. uptempo
If he really knew me, Sonia, Vernon	g-b1/b-d#1	ballad
They're playing my song, Vernon, Sonia	Bb-f1/gb-cb2	uptempo
If she really knew me reprise, Vernon, Sonia	c-d1/g-a1	ballad
Right, Sonia, Vernon, chorus	a-g1/c-g1	mod. uptempo
Just for tonight, Sonia	g#-a1	ballad
When you're in my arms, Vernon, Sonia, chorus	e-g1/e-e1	mod. uptempo
A lyricist? (To the studio), woman on tape (M)	f-bb1	ballad
I still believe in love, Sonia	e-a1	ballad
Fill in the words, Vernon, men's chorus	g-e1	mod. ballad
They're playing . . . reprise, company		uptempo

The Threepenny Opera (1959)

Music by Kurt Weill   Lyrics by Marc Blitzstein

Song title, **Character (Voice)**	**Range**	**Song Style**
The ballad of Mack the Knife, Narrator (T)	d-d1	ballad
Peachum's morning song, Peachum (Bar)	e-eb1	uptempo
Army song, Peachum, Mrs. Peachum (M)	eb-fb1/eb1-fb2	mod. ballad
Wedding song, chorus		anthem ballad
Pirate Jenny, Polly (M)	b-d2	sprightly ballad
Canon song, Macheath (T), Brown (Bar)	d#1-gb2/G#-d1	uptempo
Love song, Polly, Macheath	d#1-gb2/d#-gb1	ballad
Barbara's song, Polly	c1-f2	ballad
First Threepenny finale, Polly, Peachum, Mrs. Peachum	d#1-e2/c-e1 (opt. f1)/d#1-e2	uptempo
Polly's song, Polly	e1-c2	ballad
Tango ballad, Jenny (M), Macheath	b-f2/B-f1	uptempo tango

Ballad of an easy life, Macheath	e-f#1	ballad
Jealousy duet, Lucy (S), Polly	e1-f#2/e1-g♭2	uptempo
Second Threepenny finale, Macheath, Mrs. Peachum, chorus	d-e1/d1-e2	mod. uptempo
Useless song, Peachum	e-e1	mod. ballad
Solomon's song, Jenny	b-f2	ballad
Rest from the tomb, Macheath	e-e1	uptempo
Grave letter, Macheath	d-f1	slow ballad
Third Threepenny finale, company		mod. uptempo

Tommy (1993)

Music and Lyrics by Pete Townshend
Additional Music and Lyrics by John Entwhistle and Keith Moon

Song title, **Character (Voice)**	**Range**	**Song Style**
It's a boy, company		mod. uptempo
Twenty-one, Mrs. Walker (M), Lover (T), Mr. Walker (T)	g-c2/g-a♭1/f-a♭1	ballad
Amazing journey, Narrator (T)	a-g1	uptempo
Christmas, company		uptempo
Do you think it's alright, Mrs. Walker, Capt. Walker	e♭1-e♭2/g-e♭1	mod. uptempo
Fiddle about, Uncle Ernie (T), offstage men's chorus	G-b♭1	fast character
Cousin Kevin, Kevin (T)	c-a♭1	uptempo
Sensation, Narrator, chorus	f-a1	uptempo
Eyesight to the blind, Hawker (T), Harmonica Player (T), chorus	a-g1/c#-b1	mod. uptempo
Acid queen, Gypsy (M)	g-g2	uptempo
Pinball wizard, Lad 1 (T), Lad 2 (T), Kevin	d-c2/f#-a1/a-b1	uptempo
Go to the mirror, boy, ensemble		mod. uptempo
Tommy, can you hear me?, male ensemble		uptempo
I believe my own eyes, Mrs. Walker, Mr. Walker	a-b1/f-a1	mod. uptempo
Smash the mirror, Mrs. Walker	b-d1	uptempo, hard
I'm free, Tommy (T)	f#-b1	uptempo
Sensation reprise, Tommy, chorus	g-a1	uptempo
I'm free/Pinball wizard reprise, Tommy; Kevin and Guards incidental	e-a1	uptempo

Tommy's holiday camp, Uncle Ernie	d-f#1	mod. character
Sally Simpson, company		uptempo
Welcome, Tommy, chorus	d♭-a♭1	mod. ballad
We're not gonna take it, Tommy, chorus	d-b♭1	uptempo
Finale: See me, feel me, company		mod. uptempo

Two by Two (1970)

Music by Richard Rodgers   Lyrics by Martin Charnin

Song title, **Character (Voice)**	**Range**	**Song Style**
Why me?, Noah (T)	d-f#1 (opt. d3), some spoken	uptempo
Put him away, chorus		mod. uptempo
Something, somewhere, Japheth (T), chorus	e♭-g1	uptempo
You have got to have a rudder on the ark, Noah, Sons	Noah: B-e1/Sons: f-f#1	uptempo
Something doesn't happen, Rachael (S), Esther (M)	c#1-e2/d-c#1	ballad
An old man, Esther	b♭-c2	uptempo
Ninety again, Noah	c-a♭1	uptempo
Two by two, chorus		mod. uptempo
I do not know a day I did not love you, Japheth	d♭-g♭1	ballad
When it dries, Noah, family	c-g1	uptempo
You, Noah	B-b	ballad
The golden ram, Goldie (S)	a♭-c3	moving ballad
Poppa knows best, Noah, Japheth, Sons	e-e1/f#-d1	uptempo
I do not know . . . reprise, Rachel, Japheth	c1-d2/c-f1	ballad
As far as I'm concerned, Shem (Bar), Leah (M)	c-g1/e1-e♭2	uptempo, funny
Hey, girlie, Noah	A#-d1	ballad
The covenant, Noah	d-g1	ballad

Two Gentlemen of Verona (1971)

Music by Galt MacDermot   Lyrics by John Guare

Song title, **Character (Voice)**	**Range**	**Song Style**
Summer, summer, chorus		mod. uptempo

I love my father/That's a very interest- *ing question*, Girl No. 4 (S)	f1-f2	mod. ballad
I'd like to be a rose, Valentine (T), Proteus (Bar), chorus	c-a1/A-e1	mod. ballad
Symphony, Proteus, chorus	B♭-e♭1	ballad
I am not interested in love, Julia (M)	a-c2	ballad
Love, is that you?, Thurio (T), women's chorus incidental	g-c2	recitative
Thou hast metamorphosed me, Julia	a-g2	ballad
What does a lover pack?, Julia, Proteus	c1-e♭2/c-f1	mod. ballad
Pearls, Launce (Bar)	A-c#1	waltz ballad
I love my father reprise, Proteus	e♭-e♭1	ballad
Two gentlemen of Verona, Julia, Lucetta (M), women's chorus	both b♭-e♭2	uptempo
Follow the rainbow, company		mod. uptempo
Where's north, company		uptempo
Bring all the boys back home, Duke (Bar), chorus	c-e1	uptempo march
Who is Silvia?, Silvia (M), Valentine	d1-d2/d-d1	ballad
Love's revenge, Valentine	c-a1	ballad
To whom it may concern me, Silvia, Valentine	g-e2/G-e1	narrative ballad
Night letter, Silvia, Valentine	c1-a2/c-a1	uptempo
Love's revenge reprise, Valentine, men's chorus	c-c2	ballad
Calla lily lady, Proteus	e-g1	fast calypso
I come from the land of betrayal, Lucetta	c1-c2	mod. ballad
Thurio's samba, Thurio, Duke, chorus	c-c2/c-f1	uptempo
Hot lover, Launce, Speed (Bar)	d-g1/d-e♭1	quick dixieland
What a nice idea, Julia, chorus incidental	a-b1	ballad
Who is Silvia reprise, Proteus, chorus	d-f1	mod. ballad
Love me, Silvia, chorus	a-d2	driving ballad
Eglamour, Eglamour (Bar), Silvia incidental	B-e1	moving ballad
Kidnapped, company		uptempo
Howl, Valentine	G#-e1	mod. uptempo
What's a nice girl like her?, Proteus	c#-f#1	mod. ballad
Don't have the baby, Lucetta, Speed, Launce, Julia	men: B-c1/her: b-c2*	mod. uptempo
Milkmaid, Milkmaid (M), Launce	b-d2/c-d1	uptempo
Love has driven me sane, Silvia, company	c1-c2	mod. uptempo

Alternate for "Howl":
Mansion, Valentine   c#-f#1   ballad

*Could be performed as a solo.

The Unsinkable Molly Brown (1960)
Music and Lyrics by Meredith Willson

Song title, **Character (Voice)**	**Range**	**Song Style**
I ain't down yet, Molly (M), Brothers	bb-f2/spoken	uptempo
Belly up to the bar, boys, unison men's chorus		uptempo
Colorado, my home, Johnny (T)	B-f1	uptempo
Belly up to the bar, boys reprise, Molly, men's chorus	a-a1	uptempo
Cabin sequence, Johnny, Molly	db-f1/g-ab1	ballad
Beautiful people of Denver, Molly	f-a1	ballad
Are you sure?, Molly, chorus	f#-c2	uptempo
We're going to learn to read and write, Molly, Johnny	ab-eb2/Ab-f1	uptempo
Happy birthday, Mrs. J.J. Brown, Princess (S), chorus	a-f2	uptempo
Bon jour, ensemble	c-f1	mod. uptempo
If I knew, Johnny		ballad
Keep a-hoppin', chorus	d-e1	uptempo
Leadville Johnny Brown, Johnny	G-eb1/ab-ab1	ballad
Dolce far niente, Prince (Bar), Molly		ballad

The Vagabond King (1925)
Music by Rudolph Friml   Lyrics by Brian Hooker

Song title, **Character (Voice)**	**Range**	**Song Style**
Life is like a bubble in our glasses, company		uptempo
Love for sale, Huguette (S), chorus	eb1-g2	mod. uptempo
Drinking song, Tabary (T), chorus	d-a1	uptempo
Song of the Vagabonds, Villon (T), chorus	c-f1	mod. ballad

Some day, Katherine (S)	f#1-a2	ballad
Only a rose, Katherine, Villon	d1-g2/d-f1	ballad
Hunting, chorus		uptempo
Scotch archer's song, B solo, men's chorus	D-d1	march uptempo
To-morrow, Villon, Katherine	eb-f1/eb1-ab2	mod. uptempo
Some day, company		ballad
Nocturn, S, Bar soli, chorus	c1-bb2/c-eb1	ballad
Serenade, Tabary, Oliver, Mary (M)	c-e1/c-e1/c1-e2	waltz ballad
Huguette waltz, Huguette (S)	d1-f2	waltz ballad
Love me tonight, Katherine, Villon	c1-a2/c-e1	waltz ballad
Sons of toil and danger, company		march uptempo
Church music, Bar solo, chorus	eb-eb1	anthem ballad
Only a rose reprise, company		mod. ballad

West Side Story (1957)

Music by Leonard Bernstein   Lyrics by Stephen Sondheim

Song title, **Character (Voice)**	**Range**	**Song Style**
Jet song, Riff (Bar), Jets (male ensemble)	bb-g1	mod. uptempo, brassy
Something's coming, Tony (T)	e-f#1	jazzy ballad
Maria, Tony	b-ab1	ballad
Balcony scene, Maria (S), Tony	bb-ab2/Bb-ab1	ballad
America, Anita (M), Rosalie (M), women	both a-d1	uptempo
Cool, Riff, Jets	c#-eb1	mod. uptempo
One hand, one heart, Tony, Maria	gb-gb1/gb-ab2	ballad
Tonight, Maria, Tony, Anita, Riff, Bernardo	SMTBB	uptempo
I feel pretty, Maria, girls	c1-g2	mod. uptempo
Gee, Officer Krupke, Action (Bar), Jets	G-f1	fast character
Boy like that/I have a love, Maria, Anita	bb-bb2/f-d2	driving ballad

Where's Charley? (1948)

Music and Lyrics by Frank Loesser

Song title, **Character (Voice)**	**Range**	**Song Style**
The years before us, men's chorus		mod. ballad
Better get out of here, Amy, Kitty, Charley, Jack	SSTB	mod. ballad

Song title, Character (Voice)	Range	Song Style
The new Ashmolean marching society and students' conservatory band, company		uptempo
My darling, my darling, Jack (T), Kitty (S)	c-f1/eb1-g2	ballad
Make a miracle, Amy (S), Charley (Bar)	bb-eb2/Bb-eb1	uptempo
Serenade with asides, Spettigue (Bar)	B-c1	character ballad
Lovelier than ever, Sir Francis (T), Donna Lucia (S), chorus	d-g1/d1-g2	ballad
The woman in his room, Amy	d-fb2	waltz ballad
Pernambuco, chorus		uptempo
Where's Charley, Jack, company	d-g1	uptempo
Once in love with Amy, Charley	Bb-bb	moving ballad
The gossips, women's chorus		uptempo
The years before us reprise, men's chorus		mod. ballad
Lovelier than ever reprise, chorus		ballad
At the red rose cotillion, Jack, Kitty, chorus	d-g1/d1-g2	waltz ballad
Finale: My, darling, my darling, company		uptempo

Wildcat (1960)

Music by Cy Coleman   Lyrics by Carolyn Leigh

Song title, Character (Voice)	Range	Song Style
Oil, chorus		uptempo
Hey, look me over!, Wildy (M), Janie (M)	a-c#2/f#-e2	uptempo march
You've come home, Joe (Bar)	Bb-eb1	ballad
What takes my fancy, Sookie (Bar), Wildy	Ab-c1/ab-c2	uptempo hoe-down
You're a liar, Joe, Wildy	B-c1/c1-b1	uptempo, funny
One day we dance, Hank (T), Janie	d-fb1/c1-c2	waltz ballad
Give a little whistle, Wildy, Joe, chorus	g-c2/Bb-eb1	uptempo polka
Tall hope, Tattoo (T), Oney (Bar), men	ab-eb1/db-eb1	blues ballad
Dancing on my tippy-tippy toes, Countess (M), Wildy	a-d2/a-c#2	waltz ballad
El sombrero, Wildy, Cisco (Bar), Oney	all b-e1	uptempo
Corduroy road, Joe, chorus	Bb-eb1	uptempo
Hey, look me over reprise, company		uptempo

The Will Rogers Follies (1993)

Music by Cy Coleman   Lyrics by Betty Comden and Adolph Green

Song title, Character (Voice)	Range	Song Style
Let's go flying, chorus		uptempo
Will-a-mania, Ziegfeld's Favorite (M), chorus	g-a1	mod. uptempo
Give a man enough rope, Will (Bar), Cowboy quartet	B♭-f1	mod. ballad
It's a boy, Clem (Bar), girl's sextet	c-e1	mod. ballad
It's a boy reprise, Will	B-d1	mod. ballad
My unknown someone, Betty Blake (M)	a♭-c2	mod. ballad
The big time, Will, Betty, four children	B-d#1/b-d#2	uptempo
My big mistake, Betty; Will, incidental	f-d2	ballad
Marry me now/Without you, company		uptempo
Entr'acte, men's chorus; Will incidental		mod. uptempo
Look around, Will	c#-d1	mod. uptempo
The campaign, "Our favorite son," Will, chorus	c-e♭1	mod. uptempo
No man left for me, Betty	a-c#2	blues ballad
Presents for Mrs. Rogers, Will, Cowboy quartet	B-c#1	moving ballad
Never met a man I didn't like, Will, chorus	B-d#	moving ballad

Wish You Were Here (1952)

Music and Lyrics by Harold Rome

Song title, Character (Voice)	Range	Song Style
Camp Kare-free, chorus		uptempo
There's nothing nicer than people, Teddy (S), chorus	b♭-e♭2	uptempo
Ballad of a social director, Itchy (Bar), chorus	d-e1	fast character
Shopping around, Fay (M)	c1-b♭1	jazzy ballad
Waiter's song, men's chorus		fast, fight song
Mix and mingle, Chick (T), chorus, many soli	c-f1	uptempo
Could be, company		ballad
Light fantastic, chorus		uptempo
Where did the night go?, Chick, Teddy, chorus	c-e♭1/f1-b♭2	ballad

Certain individuals, company		uptempo
They won't know me, Chick	B-g1	ballad
Summer afternoon, Pinky (T), chorus	B#-f#1	moving ballad
Where did the night go reprise, chorus		ballad
Don Jose of Far Rockaway, Itchy, chorus	c#-eb1	tango uptempo
Everybody love everybody, Fay, company	bb-b1	uptempo
Wish you were here, Chick, background chorus	eb-ab1	ballad
Relax, Pinky, Teddy	c-eb1/mostly spoken	ballad
Gone with the night, company		be-bop uptempo
Flattery, Itchy, Teddy, chorus	c-c1/c1-c2	moving ballad
Summer afternoon, company		moving ballad

The Wiz (1975)
Music and Lyrics by Charlie Smalls

Song title, Character (Voice)	Range	Song Style
The feeling we once had, Aunt Em (M)	g-c2	gospel ballad
He's the Wiz, Addaperle (S)	f-c3	jazzy mod.
Soon as I get home, Dorothy (S)	bb-c#2	ballad
I was born on the day before yesterday, Scarecrow (T)	e-a1	uptempo
Ease on down the road, Dorothy, chorus	g-db1	uptempo
Slide some oil to me, Tinman (T)	g-bb1	mod. uptempo
Mean ole lion, Lion (T)	G-bb1	mod. uptempo
Be a lion, Dorothy, Lion	bb-db2/ab-ab1	anthem ballad
So you wanted to meet the Wizard, Wiz (T)	e-g1	driving uptempo
What would I do if I could feel, Tinman	d-a1	blues ballad
Don't nobody bring me no bad news, Evillene (M), chorus	g-db2	uptempo
Everybody rejoice ("Brand new day"), Dorothy, chorus	e-bb1	uptempo
Who do you think you are, company		mod. uptempo
Believe in yourself, Wiz	c-g1	ballad
Y'all got it, Wiz, chorus	g-a1	fast, hard jazz
A rested body, Glinda (M)	f-d2	moving ballad
When I think of home, Dorothy	g-e2	moving ballad

Woman of the Year (1981)

Music by John Kander — Lyrics by Fred Ebb

Song title, Character (Voice)	Range	Song Style
Opening, Tess (M), women's chorus	e-f1	mod. uptempo
Woman of the year, Tess, women's chorus	e-g1	mod. uptempo
See you in the funny papers, Sam (Bar)	A-d♭1	mod. uptempo
Right, Tess, Gerald (Bar)	a♭-c2/G-a	uptempo
Shut up, Gerald, Sam, Tess, Gerald	all c-c1	uptempo, funny
So what else is new?, Sam, Katz (M)	B♭-d♭1/A♭-d♭1	mod. ballad
Second poker game, male ensemble		uptempo
One of the boys, Tess, men	e-g1	mod. uptempo
Table talk, Tess, Sam	f-g1/F-g	ballad
The two of us, Sam, Tess, company	both f-b♭1	mod. ballad
It isn't working, chorus		uptempo
I told you so, Gerald, Helga (M)	B-e1/b-c#2	uptempo
Woman of the year reprise, Tess	g♭-e2	driving ballad
I wrote the book, Tess, men's chorus	b-d2	ballad
Happy in the morning, Alex (M)	a-f1	mod. ballad
Sometimes a day goes by, Sam	A-c2	ballad
The grass is always greener, Jan (M), Tess	b♭-d♭2/a♭-e♭2	mod. ballad, funny
Open the window, Tess, chorus	e-f2	uptempo
Finale: Table talk reprise, company		uptempo

Wonderful Town (1953)

Music by Leonard Bernstein — Lyrics by Betty Comden and Adolph Green

Song title, Character (Voice)	Range	Song Style
Washington Square, Guide (M), chorus	c1-e♭2	mod. uptempo
Ohio, Eileen (S), Ruth (M)	b♭-a♭2/d-a♭1	mod. ballad
100 easy ways to lose a man, Ruth	g-a1	jazzy, funny
What a waste, Baker (Bar), men's chorus	A-e1	mod. uptempo
Little bit in love, Eileen	c1-c#2	mod. ballad
Pass the football, Wreck (Bar)	A-e1	mod. character
Nice people, Eileen, chorus	d1-d3	ballad, then fast
Quiet girl, Baker, men's chorus	G-c1	ballad
Conga, Ruth, Admirals (male ensemble)	f-a♭1	uptempo

Eileen, Eileen, men's chorus, several soli	g1-g2	ballad
Swing, Ruth, chorus	e1-e2	uptempo
Ohio reprise, Eileen, Ruth	b♭-b♭1/d♭-a♭1	mod. ballad
It's love, Eileen, Baker, chorus incidental	g-c2/G-e1	uptempo
Wrong note rag, chorus; Eileen, Ruth incidental		uptempo rag
It's love reprise, Eileen, Baker, company	b-d#2/B-d1	uptempo

Working (1978)

Music and Lyrics by Stephen Schwartz, Micki Grant, Craig Carnella,
James Taylor, Graciela Daniele, Matt Landers, Susan Birkhead, Mary Rodgers

Song title, Character (Voice)	Range	Song Style
All the livelong day, company		uptempo
Lovin' Al, Al (T), chorus	B♭-f1 (one b♭1)	mod. uptempo
Newsboy, Newsboy (boy S), men's chorus	c1-d2	mod. uptempo
Nobody tells me how, Rose (S)	e1-a2	ballad
Un mejor dia vendra, Emilio (Bar), chorus	c-c1	ballad
Just a housewife, Housewife (M), chorus	a-b1	mod. ballad
Millwork, Millworker (M)	a-a1	mod. uptempo
The mason, Mason (T)	B♭-g1	ballad
If I could've been, company, many soli		mod. uptempo
It's an art, Dolores (M), chorus	a-c#2	mod. ballad
Brother trucker, Trucker (T), chorus	g-b1	rock uptempo
Joe, Joe (Bar)	d-d1	narrative ballad
Cleanin' women, Woman (M), women's chorus	b♭-e2	uptempo
Fathers and sons, Man (Bar), men's chorus incidental	c#-e1	hard ballad
Something to point to, company		driving ballad

The World Goes 'Round (1991)

Music by John Kander   Lyrics by Fred Ebb

Song title, **Character (Voice)**	**Range**	**Song Style**
And the world goes 'round, Woman 1 (M)	f#-d2	ballad
Yes, company		mod. uptempo
Coffee in a cardboard cup, company		uptempo
The happy time, Man 2 (Bar)	d#-e1	uptempo
Colored lights, Woman 3 (M)	g♭-b1	mod. ballad
Sara Lee, Man 1 (T), Women	d-g1	mod., funny
Arthur in the afternoon, Woman 2 (M)	g♭-d♭2	uptempo, funny
My coloring book, Woman 1	b♭-c2	slow waltz
I don't remember you, Man 2*	b♭-a♭1	ballad
Sometimes a day goes by, Man 1*	c-e♭1	mod. ballad
All that jazz, Woman 2, Man 1, company	g#-c2/c#-c#1	mod. fast jazz
Class, Woman 1, 3	both g♭-b1	mod. ballad
Mr. Cellophane, Man 1	b-g1	mod. ragtime
Me and my baby, company		ballad, then fast
There goes the ball game, Women	c1-g2/b-e2/g-e2	uptempo, jazzy
How lucky can you get, Woman 3, Men incidental	e-e♭2	ballad
The rink, company		mod. uptempo
Ring them bells, Woman 3, company	g#-d♭1	uptempo
Kiss of the Spider Woman, Man 2	g#-g#1	hard ballad
Only love, Woman 1 †	a-b♭1	ballad
Marry me, Man 1†	e-g♭1	ballad
A quiet thing, Woman 2†	g-e♭1	ballad
Pain, company		uptempo, funny
The grass is always greener, Women 1, 3	g-d2/g-g1	mod. ballad
We can make it, Man 2	A-f1	moving ballad
Maybe this time, Woman 1	g♭-b1	driving ballad
Isn't this better?, Woman 3	a♭-b♭1	ballad
Money, money, company		uptempo
Cabaret, company		mod. uptempo
New York, New York, company		uptempo

* These two numbers are then combined together in a quodlibet.
† These three numbers are then combined together in a quodlibet.

Your Own Thing (1968)
Music and Lyrics by Hal Hester and Danny Apolinar

Song title, Character (Voice)	Range	Song Style
No one's perfect, Viola (M), Sebastian (T)	d#1-d2/d#-e1	uptempo
The flowers, Viola	b♭-b♭1	mod. uptempo
I'm me, Danny (T), John (T), Michael (Bar): "The Apocolypse"	all c-f1	uptempo
Baby baby, Viola, Apocolypse	e1-g2/all e-g♭1	rock uptempo
Come away death, Sebastian	B♭-g♭1	ballad
I'm on my way to the top, Sebastian	f-g♭1	uptempo
Well, let it be, Olivia (M)	b♭-c2	mod. uptempo
Be gentle, Viola, Orson (Bar)	f-b1/B♭-e1	ballad
What do I know?, Viola, Apocolypse	g♭-c♭2	mod. ballad
Baby baby reprise, Sebastian, Apocolypse	f-g♭1	mambo rock
The now generation, company		march uptempo
The middle years, Sebastian	A-e1	narrative ballad
Middle years reprise, Olivia	e-c2	mod. ballad
When you're young and in love, Orson, Viola	B♭-e♭1/b♭-c2	uptempo waltz
Hunca munca, company		mambo rock
Don't leave me, Olivia, Sebastian	a-b1/A-f1	ballad
Do your own thing, Apocolypse	c-g1/c-e1/c-c1	mod. uptempo

You're a Good Man, Charlie Brown (1967)
Music and Lyrics by Clark Gesner

Song title, Character (Voice)	Range	Song Style
You're a good man, Charlie Brown, company		march uptempo
Schroeder, Lucy (S)	b#-e2	ballad
Snoopy, Snoopy (T)	G-g1	character ballad
My blanket and me, Linus (Bar)	B-e1	moving ballad
The kite, Charlie Brown (Bar)	B♭-e♭1	uptempo
The doctor is in, Lucy, Charlie	b♭-e♭2/c-f1	slow, funny
The book report, Lucy, Schroeder, Charlie, Linus	STBB	mod. ballad
The baseball game, company		uptempo
Glee club rehearsal, company		mod. ballad

Little known facts, Lucy	c1-c2	mod. uptempo
Suppertime, Snoopy	c-f#1	uptempo, jazzy
Happiness, company		mod. ballad

Zorba (1968)

Music by John Kander   Lyrics by Fred Ebb

Song title, **Character (Voice)**	**Range**	**Song Style**
Life, Leader (Bar), chorus	Bb-bb	mod. ballad
First time, Zorba (Bar)	d-e1 (much	mod. uptempo
Top of the hill, Leader, chorus	G-bb	ballad
No boom boom, Hortense (M), four admirals	g#-c#2	uptempo
Vive la difference, four admirals	unison c#-e1	uptempo
The butterfly, Nikos (T), Widow (M)	d-f1/d1-f2	mod. ballad
Goodbye Canavaro, Zorba, Hortense	G#-c#1/a#-a1	uptempo
Khania, Leader	Bb-db1	uptempo
I used to have a grandmama, Zorba	A-c#1	uptempo
Only love, Hortense	gb-bb1	ballad
Bend of the road, Leader, chorus incidental	G#-c1	mod. uptempo
Y'assou, company		uptempo
Woman, Zorba	Eb-c1	ballad
That's a beginning, Widow, Nikos	a-db2/d-f#1	ballad

Indexes

Indexes to Songs for Solo Voices

Soprano Songs

BALLADS

CHARACTER SONGS

SONGS FOR BOY SOPRANO

Mezzo-Soprano Songs

UPTEMPO SONGS

BALLADS

Tenor Songs

UPTEMPO SONGS

BALLADS

CHARACTER SONGS

Tommy's holiday camp, 142

Tramp, tramp, tramp, 94
Ze English language, 88

Bass Songs

UPTEMPO SONGS

Abie, baby, 61
All aboard for Broadway, 54
Amsterdam, 69
Any day now day, 12
Aquarius, 61
Armorer's song, 121
Ballad of the robbers, 75
Be back soon, 101
Beautiful through and through, 134
Bend of the road, 153
Blob, The, 86
Bored, 26
Born to hand jive, 59
Bring all the boys back home, 143
Brother, beware, 46
Bum's opera, 112
By Strauss, 56
Bye bye baby, 53
Cabaret, The, 47
Calla lily lady, 143
Camelot, 21
Campaign, The, 147
Celebration, 26
Chava sequence, 44
Cinderella, darling, 64
Colored spade, 61
Come along with me, 22
Come back to me, 102
Comedy tonight, 53
Contini submits, 96
Cool, 145
Corduroy road,146
Cradle will rock, The, 33
Crow, The, 153
Dancing is everything, 139
Dear world, 36

Dentist, 80
Dipsey's comin' over, 139
Do it the hard way, 108
Doing the reactionary, 111
Don Jose of Far Rockaway, 148
Don't give up so easy, 57
Don't marry me, 48
Don't rain on my parade, 52
Early in the morning, 46
Epiphany, 136
Every day is ladies day with me, 117
Everybody ought to have a maid, 53
Everybody says don't, 7
Everybody today is turnin' on, 66
Everybody's gotta be somewhere, 29
First time, 153
Fish, 8
Flair, 130
For sweet charity, 138
Forest ranger, The, 77
Funeral tango, 69
G-man song, The, 111
Get me to the church on time, 91
Gigi, 55
Give my regards to Broadway, 54
God-why-don't-you love-me blues,
    The, 49
Gospel according to King, The, 91
Gotta be this or that, 50
Grand canal, The, 96
Great big town, A, 108
Guido's song, 96
Half as big as life, 116
Happy hunting horn, 108
Happy time, The, 151
Hey there, fans, 130
How sad, 98

BALLADS

Index to Duets

Duets for Two Women

UPTEMPO SONGS

Above the law (MM), 6

America (MM), 145

Apple doesn't fall, The (MM), 118

Behave yourself (MM), 117

Bistro, The (SS), 110

Bosom buddies (MM), 82

Cinderella at the grave (SM), 67

Climbing over rocky mountains (SS), 113

Don't ah ma me (MM), 118

Every little nothing (SM), 77

Funny (MM), 91

Furs and feathers (SM), 87

Hey, look me over! (MM), 146

I may want to remember today (SM), 129

If momma was married (SS), 60

It's me (MM), 84

It's possible (SM), 29

Jealousy duet (SM), 141

Joke, The (MM), 91

Leave it to the girls (MM), 6

Marry the man today (SM), 60

Melody de Paris (SS), 110

Mother, angel, darling (MM), 68

Motherhood march (MM), 63

Mrs. A (MM), 118

No lies (MM), 15

Oh, you wonderful boy (MM), 76

Stepsister's lament (MM), 29

Strong woman number (MM), 66

Take him (MM), 108

This is as good as it gets (SM), 57

Two gentlemen of Verona (MM), 143

We'll always be bosom buddies (MM), 69

BALLADS

About a quarter to nine (MM), 52

Baby, dream your dream (MM), 137

Biggest ain't the best, The (SM), 98

Boy like that, A (SM), 145

Can't help lovin' dat man (SM), 126

Carnegie Hall pavane (MM), 102

Class (SM), 28; (MM), 151

Dancing on my tippy-tippy toes (MM), 146

Every day a little death (SM), 79

Footsteps (SM), 58

Grass is always greener, The (MM), 149, 151

I don't know his name (SM), 124

I have a love (SM), 145

I know him so well (MM), 27

If you don't mind my saying so (SM), 90

Indian maiden's lament (SS), 103

It's never that easy (SM), 31

I'm glad to see you got what you want (SM), 26

I've been here before (SM), 31

Just a coupl'a sisters (MM), 99

Kiss her now (MM), 70

Like him (MM), 139

Little Mary Sunshine (SS), 77

Little me (MM), 78

Love makes the world go round (MM), 98

Lullaby (SM), 132

Nowadays (MM), 28

Duets for Two Men

Mamie is Mimi (TT), 54
Man of la Mancha (TB), 82
Maybe my baby (TB), 58
Middle class (TB), 69
Most happy fella, The (BB), 88
Mover's life, A (BB), 66
Muddy water (TB), 15
Mushnik and son (TB), 80
My one and only (BB), 92
My way (TB), 119
Never say no (BB), 43
No contest (TT), 27
Now (It's just the gas) (TB), 80
On the side of the angels (BB), 45
One indispensable man, The, 74
One who's run away, The (BB), 62
Penniless bums (BB), 133
Persuasion, The (BB), 22
Plant a radish (BB), 43
Poor tied up darlin' (TT), 120
Poppa knows best (TT), 143
Raquetball II (TB), 42
Right track (TT), 113
Rock and roll party queen (TT), 59
Simon Zealots, poor Jerusalem, 70
Stouthearted men (TB), 95
Sweet beginnings (TB), 119
Take me along (BB), 138
There ain't nobody here but us
    chickens (TB), 47
There's nowhere to go but up! (BB),
    74
Things to remember, 118
Thrill of first love (TB), 83
Thurio's samba (TB), 143
Tinker's song (TB), 121
Typical self-made American (TB),
    132
Unofficial spokesman (TT), 132
What causes that? (TB), 33
When the sun goes down in the
    South (TB), 15
Where would you be without me
    (TB), 119

Wonderful day like today, A (TB),
    118
Yankee doodle (TB), 77
You did it (BB), 91
You're nothing without me (TB), 29

BALLADS
Agony (BB), 67
At night she comes home to me
    (TB), 11
Ballad of Booth, The (TB), 9
Beauty that drives men mad, The
    (BB), 133
Blob, The/Good thing going (TB),
    86
Chess game, The (TB), 83
Dear home of mine (TB), 32
Doin' it for Sugar (BB), 134
Fanny (TB), 43
Father to son (TB), 83
Four black dragons (TB), 106
Geraniums in the winder (TB), 24
Golden days (TB), 133
Good thing going (TB), 86
Harrigan (TB), 55
He won't be happy till he gets it
    (BB), 10
I can see it (TB), 43
I don't remember you (TB), 151
I like you (TB), 42
In the days gone by (TT), 32
Interrogation scene—Simple (BB),
    6
It would have been wonderful (BB),
    79
It's legitimate (TT), 38
I'd like to be a rose (TB), 143
Last supper, The (TT), 71
Letters (TT), 81
Lily's eyes (TB), 123
Lovely (TB), 53
Man to man talk (BB), 105
Meilinki meilchik (TB), 130
Mine (TT), 103
No more (BB), 67

Duets for a Man and a Woman

UPTEMPO SONGS

Young and healthy (MT), 51
Your majesties (MT), 28
You're a liar (MB), 146
You're nearer (ST), 9

BALLADS
Ain't no party (ST), 39
All at once (ST), 9
All the children in a row (MB), 118
All the dearly beloved (MB), 65
All 'er nothin' (ST), 101
Almost like being in love (SB), 18
Always, always you (MB), 24
And what if we had loved like that
    (MB), 11
Angelus, The (ST), 138
Another wedding song (MB), 31
Any moment (MB), 67
Anyone would love you (MB), 37
Apukad eros kezen (MB), 27
Army song (MB), 140
As simple as that (ST), 87
As on the seasons we sail (MB), 127
At the red rose cotillion (ST), 146
Baby, baby, baby (MB), 11
Balcony/Casa Rosada (SB), 41
Balcony scene (ST), 145
Barcelona (ST), 31
Be a lion (ST), 148
Be gentle (MB), 152
Beautiful (MT), 135
Because you're you (MB), 117
Before and after (MB), 10
Beguine (MT), 34
Bess, you is my woman (SB), 115
Best of times, The (MB), 20
Better than a dream (MT), 13
Boy wanted (MB), 92
Boys and girls like you and me
    (MT), 28
Breakfast over sugar (MB), 83
Breeze kissed your hair, The (MT),
    25
But not for me (MB), 56
Butterfly, The (MT), 153

By a goon-a (MB), 57
By my side (MB), 57
By the sea (MB), 136
Cabin sequence (MT), 144
Call of love (ST), 32
Carried away (MT), 102
Changes (SB), 6
Choo choo honeymoon (MB), 34
Colorado love call (SB), 77
Colors of my life, The (MT), 12
Come to my garden (ST), 123
Coquette (MT), 54
Could we start again, please (MT),
    71
Cricket on the hearth, The (ST), 138
Croon (MT), 32
Cry the beloved country (MT), 80
C'est magnifique (MT), 22
Dear little cafe (MT), 16
Desert song, The (ST), 36
Dice are rolling (SB), 41
Did you close your eyes? (SB), 95
Do I love you because you're
    beautiful (ST), 29
Do you love me? (MB), 44
Doctor is in, The (SB), 152
Do-do-do (ST), 100
Don't forget the lilac bush (ST), 132
Don't leave me (MT), 152
Don't look at me (MB), 49
Embraceable you (MT), 56
Evermore and a day (MT), 16
Everything's alright (MT), 71
Fact can be a beautiful thing, A
    (MB), 116
First letter (SB), 109
Flattery (SB), 148
Flower garden of my heart, The
    (MB), 108
Forbidden love (MB), 8
Forever yours (MT), 105
Forty-five minutes from Broadway
    (MB), 54
From this day on/Farewell (SB), 18
Funny face (MB), 92

Index to Trios

BALLADS

Index to
Quartets and Small Ensembles

Index to
Choruses and Company Numbers

Women's Choruses

Children's Choruses

UPTEMPO CHORUSES

Beautiful land, 119
Catch me if you can, 131
Consider yourself, 101
Food, glorious food, 101
I whistle a happy tune, 72
It's the hard-knock life, 4
Schoolroom scene, 72
So long, farewell, 128
That's what it is to be young, 119
Torreadorables, 60
Very funny funeral, A, 119

SLOWER CHORUSES

Getting to know you, 72
I got me, 6
My favorite things, 128
Other woman, The, 6
Santa Evita, 41
Sound of music, The, 128

Men's Choruses

UPTEMPO CHORUSES

After all these years, 118
Aggie song, The, 15
Auctioneer's song, 120
Back to work, 111
Belly up to the bar, boys, 144
Benjamin calypso, 72
Best of times, The, 21
Bloody Mary, 129
Boys, The, 15
Chase, The, 18
Come sir, will you join?, 133
Credit's due to me, The, 47
Drinking song, 133
Every once in a while, 37
Farmer Jacob lay a-snoring, 133
Flying, 92
Footman's chorus, 88
Forest rangers, 78
Game, The, 35
Gesticulate, 73
Grapes of Roth, 116
Heart, 34
Hello, Dolly, 63
Hey, there, good times, 66

I'm on my way, 107
Join the Navy, 63
La cage aux folles, 21
Let us sing a song, 133
Let's put him in the stocks, 121
Look for the woman, 12
Luck be a lady, 60
Make way, 8
Never, never be an artist, 30
New Orleans jeunesse doreé, 94
Oh, better far to live and die, 113
Oh, cherrily sounds the hunter's
   horn, 121
Oh see the little lambkins play, 121
Oldest established, The, 60
On a lopsided bus, 112
One more angel in heaven, 71
Pirate's march, 110
Politics and poker, 45
Rink, The 118
Rock Island, 90
Scotch archer's song, 145
Scream, 66
Search, The, 80
Second poker game, 149

Mixed Voices

SLOWER CHORUSES

Index to
Composers and Lyricists

Appendix: Publishers' Addresses

Music Theatre International
545 8th Ave.
New York, NY 10018

Rogers and Hammerstein Theatre Library
Amateur Rights:
      229 W. 28th St., 11th Floor
      New York, NY 10001
Professional Rights:
      1633 Broadway, Suite 3801
      New York, NY 10019-6746

Samuel French, Inc.
45 W. 25th St.
New York, NY 10010-2751

Tams-Witmark Music Library, Inc.
560 Lexington Ave.
New York, NY 10022

About the Author

David P. DeVenney is founder and music director of Vocal-BAROQUE, a professional chamber choir in Columbus, Ohio, and music director of the Reading Choral Society in Reading, Pennsylvania. He is a member of the music faculty of West Chester University, where he conducts the Concert Choir and University Chorale, and teaches courses in choral conducting and literature, and musical theatre history. Prior to West Chester, Dr. DeVenney taught at Otterbein College, Virginia Tech, and The University of Arizona. He holds degrees in music from Iowa State University, the University of Wisconsin-Madison, and the College-Conservatory of Music, University of Cincinnati.

In addition to his active performance schedule, Dr. DeVenney is the author of numerous books, including a four-volume reference series on American choral music, *The Chorus in Opera* (Scarecrow Press), and a volume of *Source Readings in American Choral Music*. He has also written nearly two dozen articles on topics in choral music ranging from Schütz to Brahms.